Anonymous

Christian Unity and the Bishops' Declaration

lectures delivered in 1895 under the auspices of the Church Club of New York

Anonymous

Christian Unity and the Bishops' Declaration
lectures delivered in 1895 under the auspices of the Church Club of New York

ISBN/EAN: 9783337262310

Printed in Europe, USA, Canada, Australia, Japan

Cover: Foto ©Lupo / pixelio.de

More available books at **www.hansebooks.com**

THE CHURCH CLUB LECTURES.

Uniform red cloth. Price, per volume, 50c. net; by post, 60c.

1888.—THE HISTORY AND TEACHING OF THE EARLY CHURCH, as a Basis for the Re-Union of Christendom By Bishops COXE and SEYMOUR, and the Rev. Drs. RICHEY, GARRISON, and EGAR.

1889.—THE CHURCH IN THE BRITISH ISLES. Sketches of its Continuous History from the Earliest Times to the Restoration. By Bishops DOANE and KINGDON, and the Rev. Drs. HART, ALLEN, and GAILOR.

1890.—THE POST-RESTORATION PERIOD OF THE CHURCH IN THE BRITISH ISLES. In continuation of the volume for 1889. By Bishops PERRY and McLAREN, Ven. Dr. DAVENPORT, and the Rev. Drs. MORTIMER and RICHEY.

1891.—CATHOLIC DOGMA. The Fundamental Truths of Revealed Religion. By Bishops LITTLEJOHN and SESSUMS, the Rev Drs. HUNTINGTON, MORTIMER, and ELLIOTT, and the Rev Prof. WALPOLE.

1892.—THE CHURCH'S MINISTRY OF GRACE. By Bishops GARRETT and GRAFTON, the Very Rev. Dr. ROBBINS, and the Rev. Drs. CLARK and FISKE.

1893.—THE SIX ŒCUMENICAL COUNCILS OF THE UNDIVIDED CATHOLIC CHURCH. By Bishop LEONARD, the Rev. Drs. DIX, ELMENDORF and RILEY, and the Revs. R. M. BENSON and W. McGARVEY.

1894.—THE RIGHTS AND PRETENSIONS OF THE ROMAN SEE. By Bishops PARET and HALL, the Rev. Dr. WATERMAN, and the Revs. GREENOUGH WHITE, ROBERT RITCHIE, and ALGERNON SIDNEY CRAPSEY.

E. & J. B. YOUNG & CO.

COOPER UNION, FOURTH AVE., NEW YORK.

Christian Unity

AND THE

Bishops' Declaration

𝔏ectures

DELIVERED IN 1895 UNDER THE AUSPICES OF THE
CHURCH CLUB OF NEW YORK

NEW YORK
E. & J. B. YOUNG & CO.
COOPER UNION, FOURTH AVENUE
1895

CONTENTS.

LECTURE I.

CHRISTIAN UNITY—THE MASTER'S WORD AND THE CHURCH'S ACT 1

By the Rt. Rev. Thomas F. Gailor, D.D., Assistant Bishop of Tennessee.

LECTURE II.

THE HOLY SCRIPTURES AS THE RULE AND ULTIMATE STANDARD OF FAITH . . . 41

By the Rev. Charles E. W. Body, D.D., D C.L., Professor of Old Testament Literature and Interpretation, in the General Theological Seminary.

LECTURE III.

THE TWO CREEDS 79

By Ven. Charles S. Olmsted, of Cooperstown, N. Y., Archdeacon of the Susquehanna.

LECTURE IV.

THE TWO GREAT SACRAMENTS 119

By Ven. A. St. J. Chambré, D.D., of Lowell, Mass., Archdeacon of Lowell and Dean of Convocation.

LECTURE V.

THE HISTORIC EPISCOPATE 147

By the Rev. Francis J. Hall, M.A., Instructor of Theology in the Western Theological Seminary, Chicago, Ill.

INTRODUCTION.

THIS volume of Lectures on Christian Unity follows in natural order the volume of 1893, on the Councils of the Undivided Church, and the volume of 1894, on the Papal Schism. But it has happened further that the Lectures of 1895 have proved to be most fortunate in point of timeliness. While they were in course of delivery a remarkable revival of interest in the subject occurred, manifest on every hand in secular as well as in religious newspapers, and scarce were they concluded when the pulpits dealt with the topic on Whitsun-Day. Now, as they are going through the press, the League of Catholic Unity, composed of representatives from seven of the principal religious bodies, has put forth its circular, beginning in the following terms:

In view of the growing desire for Church unity, we, whose names are subscribed, devoutly seeking the Divine guidance and blessing, hereby associate ourselves as a league for the promotion of Catholic unity.

Without detaching ourselves from the Christian bodies to which we severally belong, or intending to compromise our relations thereto, or seeking to interfere with other efforts for Christian unity, we accept, as worthy of the most thoughtful consideration, the four principles of Church unity proposed by the Bishops of the Protestant Episcopal Church, at Chicago, in 1886, and amended by the Lambeth Conference of 1888.

We believe that upon the basis of these four principles as articles of agreement the unification of the Christian denominations of this country may proceed, cautiously and steadily, without any alteration of their existing standards of doctrine, polity, and worship which might not reasonably be made in a spirit of brotherly love and harmony, for the sake of unity and for the furtherance of all the great ends of the Church of Christ on earth.

In order to promote Catholic unity we recommend, as proposed by the Lambeth Conference, that these articles be carefully studied in connection with "the authoritative standards of doctrine, worship and government adopted by the different bodies of Christians into which the English-speaking races are divided"; and to this end we reverently and lovingly invoke the countenance and aid of the Bishops of the Protestant Episcopal Church and of all other Catholic Bishops and Christian ministers of every order and name.

May our united prayers be so blended with the prevalent intercession of our ascended Lord that we shall all become one in Him, for the glory of His Eternal Father, for the good of His Church, and for the redemption of the world!

It is therefore with great confidence that the Church Club of New York presents the volume of 1895 to the judgment of all Christian men, being assured not only of the importance of the subject which it treats, but also that the public mind is now directed to that subject with peculiar attention. The learned Lecturers appeal alike to the intellect and the affections of their separated brethren in Christ, and it may not be too much to hope at this time that both mind and heart shall be engaged by their words; a man need not be a Churchman to be touched by the pathetic giving up of things human in the Bishops' offer of 1886: "That in all things of human ordering or human choice, relating to modes of worship and discipline, or to traditional customs, this Church is ready in the spirit of love and humility to forego all preferences of her own."

Bishop Gailor's remark is that: "To denounce this Declaration of the Bishops as a sectarian effort of the Protestant Episcopal Church to absorb other Christian denominations, or to look upon the movement as anything else than unselfish, generous, and full of the spirit of Christ, is to confess to blind prejudice and real indifference to the reunion of the Christian world." And it is simply and literally true, as he says, that a single proposition of it "exacts of Churchmen more of generous sacrifice both of preference and conviction than the agreement to the whole Declaration would require from any other body of Christian people." These utterances are the key-note of the present volume.

It remains for the Church Club to fix here a record of its deep obligation to the accomplished Lecturers of 1895 - Bishop Gailor, Archdeacons Chambré and Olmsted, the Rev. Dr. Body, and the Rev. Francis J. Hall—for their generous labors.

New York, July 21, 1895.

Christian Unity—The Master's Word and the Church's Act.

LECTURE I.

THE RT. REV. THOMAS F. GAILOR, D.D
Assistant Bishop of Tennessee.

CHRISTIAN UNITY—THE MASTER'S WORD AND THE CHURCH'S ACT.

IT is a depressing experience to visit a town of 1,800 inhabitants, where perhaps 500 people attend church on Sunday, and to find that there are ten or twelve rival churches in the place, bidding for the patronage of these five hundred people; and that the expense of maintaining this multitude of sects is so great that no denomination can afford to have a resident minister. Yet this is getting to be a not uncommon ecclesiastical condition in many Eastern and Southern towns. It is not to be wondered at, under the circumstances, that a large proportion of the community are non-church-goers, that the great majority are indifferent, and that there is no religious provision for works of practical charity. There are large districts in this country where religion flourishes after a certain fashion, and where yet a free hospital, or a free home, well-conducted and under Christian influences, for the poor, the aged, the infirm, is almost unknown.

The United States Census Report for 1890 gives a list of 128 Christian denominations, with fifteen non-Christian and 156 unattached congregations. These denominations represent differences of doctrinal belief and practice on almost every article of the Christian faith. The Divinity of JESUS Christ, the Atonement, the value and meaning of the Sacraments, the nature and destiny of man, the nature of God, the inspiration and design and contents of the Bible, the form and purpose of public worship; each and all of these great themes are subjects of serious, and, in some instances, of fierce and intolerant, dissension. Even the subtlest metaphysical speculations, and the simplest variations in taste and temperament, are the bases on which, for reasons of conscience, Christian men and women separate themselves for their habitual worship.

There are those who use musical instruments and those who do not. There are those who sing hymns and those who sing psalms. There are " The old Two-Seed in the Spirit Predestinarian"; and there are the "Defenceless"; "The Free Will"; the "United"; "The Separatists"; the "Reformed"; "The Associate Reformed"; "The

Primitive"; "The Independent" and "The Reorganized."

Although there are Christian houses of worship in the United States with a seating capacity of 44,000,000, valued at $680,000,000, there are only 20,000,000 members reported, and of these, 1,000,000 are divided into 103 denominations, varying in size from 100 to 100,000 members each, holding more than $66,000,000 worth of property, the annual interest on which would support more than 4,000 missionaries in the foreign or domestic field.

Meanwhile, sixty-eight per cent. of the population of the United States, or more than 44,000,000 of people, are reported as without any religious affiliation whatever. And infidelity—the infidelity that represents intellectual scepticism and the infidelity that represents spiritual indifference or despair, and the infidelity that represents moral failure—infidelity continues to be aggressive and widespread. Crime is increasing more rapidly than the population. Our improved educational facilities, of which we are justly proud, have enabled criminals to become intellectually sharper, more enterprising, and more successful. The amount of money publicly known to have been lost by embezzlements and robberies for 1894 was $25,234,112, as compared with $19,929,692 for 1893. Official corruption and commercial dishonesties and social falsehoods have become so common that confidence, that surest foundation of the prosperity of States, is rare between man and man, and the business of the country feels the creeping palsy of that anti-Christ that maketh and worketh a lie. The chill of uncertainty affects our missionary work at home and abroad. The Chinese write articles in our own reviews demanding to know why we ask the Chinese to become Christians, when we ourselves seem to be unable to determine what Christianity is.

But worse than this: Our seemingly utter inability to agree together on any rational statement of the Christian religion has led many men and women to the conclusion that after all the Christian Gospel is not a definite message of help and blessing to mankind, but that it is a force or influence—vague and indefinable—representing the highest spiritual aspiration of the race and including in its cloudy and indistinct and diffusive atmosphere everything that man thinks or imagines to be good and true. Therefore, whatever fancy or theory or interpretation seems to any man or woman to be the sufficient explanation of life's problems, this is straightway labelled Christianity and supported by appeal to the Christian Scriptures. We have lived to see Buddhism, Gnosticism, Sabellianism, Docetism, Occultism, each claiming to be the true Christian Gospel, and many simple Christians utterly unable to refute the claim.

In the fear and love then of JESUS Christ Our Lord Who died and rose again for us and Who shall come to judge; in distress before the increasing boldness of confident unbelief and ostentatious sin; in shame over the pitiful contentions of the sects of Christendom—every earnest believer must ask himself: (1) Whether it was the purpose of Christ that these divisions should exist; (2) How these divisions were brought about; and (3) What, in faith and love and reason, can be done to end the strife.

Our Lord's recorded words in His prayer for His people are the standing challenge to those who confound unity with uniformity, and undertake to justify the present divisions as not inconsistent with the progress of the Gospel. "That they all may be one; as Thou, Father, art in Me, and I in Thee, that they also may be one in us: that the world may believe that Thou hast sent Me" (St. John xvii. 21). It is a constantly recurring thought in St. Paul's epistles. The missionary enthusiasm of the first Christians, their patience in suffering, their hopeful endurance of persecution, their generous philanthropy and active charity, their very moral earnestness,—was influenced and strengthened by the conviction that there was "One Lord, one faith, one baptism, One God and Father of all" (Eph. iv. 5, 6); that they, "being many, were one body in Christ, and every one members one of another" (Rom. xii. 5). It was the farewell message of St. John. Ignatius in Syria appeals to it, and Irenæus in Gaul assumes it as the characteristic of the Christian system. And as a matter of fact it was realized in the early Church. The unity existing in the middle of the third century was a visible and potent and intelligible unity, quite compatible with individual development and free institutions. It was not based upon rigid and mechanical and technical statements of doctrine, for the Creed professed was the simplest expression of the great facts of the Gospel, viz.: Belief in God the Father and His forgiveness; in God the Son and our resurrection through Him, and in God the Holy Ghost and His everlasting life; and making these saving truths real, actual, practical, in human experience here and now: Belief in the Kingdom of Christ, the Holy Catholic Church. This unity admitted of wide diversity in the ritual and modes of worship of the various Dioceses. It was not incompatible with great variety of speculative belief and of practical administration. But it was a unity with tremendous power for good, because it rested on the fact of the Incarnation, and the soul's contact with the Incarnate One, through the means of grace and help conveyed in the One Body.

It was during the reign of this unity that

Cyprian was able to say of the whole Church that "the Church, flooded with the light of the Lord, puts forth her rays through the whole world, with yet one light, which is spread upon all places, while its unity of body is not infringed. She stretches forth her branches over the earth in the riches of plenty, and pours abroad her bountiful and onward streams, yet is there one Head, one Source, one Mother, abundant in the results of her fruitfulness" (*De unitat. Eccl.* 4). It was in the vigor of this corporate unity that the Church survived all persecutions, and conquered the Roman Empire and set the cross of Christ on the palaces of kings. It was this that met the shock of barbarian invasions, converted the conquerors, and saved the civilization of Europe from complete destruction. It was before this unity was entirely subverted by Papal imperialism that the great missionary conquests of the Church were achieved and the nations of Europe became Christian nations; and it is a significant fact that no great people has been converted to Christianity since that original unity of the Church was lost.

The story of that loss is the saddest chapter in Ecclesiastical History. I shall not elaborate it, because it was told with wealth of learning and research to the Church Club last year. Of course it was not a swift and sudden revolution, but a gradual assumption and concentration of authority in the Roman See. The men who, one after another, brought it about, were not intentionally disloyal to the past. On the contrary, they acted, as a rule, according to their conscientious convictions. History was not an open book to them. Grave and serious evils threatened to rob the Church of her spiritual character and authority; and they felt the necessity of opposing a spiritual absolutism to the secular absolutism that menaced the Church's life. I say this much for Hildebrand and his predecessors. And yet under Hildebrand's influence in 1054 the unity was broken by the schism between the East and West; and under Hildebrand's dominion, as Gregory VII., in 1080, the old idea of unity was abandoned in the organization of the new Papal Empire. The revolution under Hildebrand, for it was a revolution, is the greatest epoch in Church History before the Reformation. By him and his immediate successors between 1074 and 1300 a new Secular Power, fenced about and guarded with spiritual sanctions, lifted its head above all dominions of the world. It claimed authority over all earthly kingdoms and " exacted an allegiance on oath," as Phillimore says (*International Law*, p. 203), " far above that which the municipal law of any country could impose or any temporal sovereign could enforce." It collected feudal revenues and created and carried on its own Department of State. It claimed for its official representatives in various countries a peculiar status and separate rights. Under this new *régime* the Roman Pontiff claimed the title Pope to the exclusion of all other Bishops. The enforced celibacy of the clergy created a disciplined army of officers loyal to the one ruler and detached from ordinary human interests. The Popes ceased to date their acts from the years of the reign of the Emperor, or to stamp their coins with his impress. The power of excommunication was no longer limited to spiritual offences, but was extended to secular affairs. And the glory of the new Empire reached its zenith in Boniface VIII., whose bull, "*Unam Sanctam*," declares that all temporal as well as all spiritual power is in the Church, and excommunicates any secular judge who presumes to interfere in criminal cases against ecclesiastical persons.

We are not discussing here the truth or falsity, the strength or weakness, of the Mediæval system, as an interpretation of the Christian Gospel. It was part of God's providential order in history, and the poor and oppressed found in it often a merciful relief from feudal tyranny. But two results, or at least two coincident tendencies, are very evident. During the period after Hildebrand, the tendency to define doctrine in scholastic fashion ran unchecked. The dogma of transubstantiation and the rule of compulsory confession were declared in 1215. The new doctrine of Purgatory took definite shape and the practice of pardons and indulgences became common. And the genius of the time was for organization, for the objective and the external. The power of the Pope and the sanctity of his office became so overshadowing, so compelling and immediate, that men forgot that there ever had been an ante-Hildebrandine constitution. The doctrine of the Apostolical Succession in its real constitutional sense, *i.e.*, that each Bishop by virtue of his consecration receives his authority from God to minister and rule, was practically denied. Augustine Triumphus in 1350, in his book on the Papal power, asserts that the Pope alone is the recipient of authority from God and that the Pope is entitled to the honor due to God, but only ministerially. John Gerson, Chancellor of the University of Paris, 1409, plaintively declares that "we have only painted images of Bishops" (*Giesler*, iv. 131). And as late as the Council of Trent, the Spanish Bishops strove in vain for a recognition of the delegated apostolic authority in the Episcopate independent of the Pope.

Thus, when the tide of the Reformation came, the Reformers began the movement with a faulty and inadequate conception of the constitution of the Church; with an inherited prejudice in favor of a legal, theological system, and a fierce dislike of the whole institutional idea of Christianity. The creed-makers of the Reformation, either from necessity or indifference, did not attempt to go back of the Mediæval system and revive a constitution that obtained in earlier ages. They simply swept away the authority of the Church altogether and replaced it with the absolute and unrelated authority of the Bible. As Beard says, "Christianity had always been presented to them by the Mediæval Church as a system of reasoned religious truth, complete in all its parts, and they could not conceive of it in any other way" (*Hib. Lect.*, 266). They were as exact and as technical in their system of logical and minute detail as the schoolmen were; and they substituted for a vast and symmetrical and minute system of dogma, based on the Bible and the witness of antiquity and tradition, another system, quite as minute if not so symmetrical, based on their interpretation of the Bible without regard to antiquity. It is safe to say that the constitution of the Church and the authority of the Church as taught and held in the age of the first Council of Nicæa had no fair and full consideration from the men who made the creeds and inaugurated the ecclesiastical systems of the sixteenth century. In their minds apparently the Mediæval Church with its manifest defects and offences was the only historical ecclesiastical system possible. It seemed to them that the only possible Bishops were the secularized ecclesiastical barons—too often self-indulgent and unspiritual—who held the rule over them in the Holy Roman Empire; and they had been taught by the extreme Papalists to regard these ecclesiastics as a degree and not an order in the ministry and little more than appendages to the Pope. Bishop Burnet, 200 years ago, said that the theory of parity of orders was the very dregs of Popery. To the Protestant the only ecclesiastical unity was a hard, monarchical absolutism, fenced about with the mazes of the Canon Law and innumerable decisions; and to this very day it is not uncommon to hear the challenge, even from prominent religious teachers, that a belief in the historical succession of authority in the Episcopate, in any sense, means nothing less than Popery. Yet the Augsburg Confession more than once declares that if Bishops were only chief ministers of the Word and Sacraments (perhaps an impossible thing in their opinion!) "the Churches ought" not only "to render obedience to them," but "by divine right." But as practically infallible potentates, with power of the sword, lording it over God's heritage, the conscience of men could not tolerate them.

What the Swiss and German Reformers rejected then was not visible unity, or Catholic unity, but the Mediæval uniformity—not Bishops, but secularized Bishops—not the ancient Constitution of the Church, but the Mediæval Constitution.

The result, however, was that they broke completely with the Mediæval Church, and in so doing cut themselves off purposely, advisedly, from external continuity with the past. The Bible was the sole appeal for doctrine, and reverence for it was the only connecting link with primitive Christianity. In theory each man was privileged to get his theology by his own reading of Scripture, and in theory the Bible was so plain that all men who would read it aright would find the same teaching as to the fundamental truths of the Gospel. In practice, however, this was found to be delusive, for Socinus, who denied the Divinity of Christ, read the Bible as carefully as Luther and Calvin, who asserted it. There is some truth in the Unitarian contention that the Continental Reformers arbitrarily refused to carry out their principles to their logical conclusion, and stopped short from timidity or from inherited scrupulosity from entirely abandoning the ancient definitions of the faith. Little by little, as was natural, doctrine, orthodox doctrine, which meant the accepted confessions of the two great schools, became the basis of whatever unity survived. Doctrine became the test of the Church's continuity. The historic Church was no longer a succession of human beings in an organized society persisting from age to age, but it was a succession often interrupted by breaks of many years—a succession of beliefs and opinions; and the people who at any period in the past were thought to have held views similar to those of the Reformers were regarded as members of the true Church, and all others were excluded. In other words, Christianity became a system of doctrines instead of an institution. This led to the theory of an invisible Church. When Cyprian spoke of the Church he meant the outward, visible, organized Church, consisting of all the baptized, the net that held fish both good and bad. When the later Reformers spoke of the Church they meant the invisible and unknown number of the elect who are saved and known only to God, or, as the Scotch Confession puts it, "the one company and multitude of men chosen of God, who rightly worship and embrace Him by true faith in JESUS Christ . . . the communion not of profane persons, but of saints . . . invisible, known only to God." In their view all visible Christian societies are only imperfect associations for the spread of the true faith, and are not churches, except in a secondary sense.

All these features, though in a different form, appear in the system of John Calvin at Geneva, which was destined to become the dominant influence in the Protestant world. Calvin, a layman himself, broke consciously and utterly with the Mediæval and ancient Church, and the external form and visible continuity of the Church were nothing to him as principles. When we read of the enthusiastic and intolerant devotion of his followers to the Genevan discipline this seems to be a contradiction. But really it was not. The root-principle of Calvin's position was that the existing Church was thoroughly corrupt and that he himself was directly and immediately called of God. And this conviction in his own mind and in the minds of his disciples was reinforced by his truly remarkable and scholastic system of doctrines, which was given to the world in his "Institutes" when he was only twenty-seven years of age, and which never underwent any serious change. Thus, in his *Reply to Sadolet* (p. 39), he admitted without hesitation that he did not have the ancient discipline of the Church, but maintained that as Jeremiah and Ezekiel and other prophets were raised up by God without the customary regular appointment, so was he called to preach the truth to an abandoned age. The doctrine was everything; the form of government was an accident. This accounts for the fact that he was quite willing to recognize, and indeed endorsed, the Episcopal government in England, and in his commentary on Titus (*Arg.*) declared that the Apostles had delegated their Apostolic authority to other men. It was not a question with him of order, but of doctrine. He made up his own mind that the original scriptural organization of the congregation was Presbyterian, and this system he established at Geneva—not because he wished to impose it upon all people and all churches, but because his own clear intelligence made him avoid the uncertainty of Lutheranism by providing for the permanence and authority of definite organization. It was Calvin's successors who claimed for the system an exclusive divine right, and they did so because, first of all, Calvin, who was an inspired man, had designed it, and secondly, because it was found in practice to be the only system in which the doctrine could be maintained. It should never be forgotten that the all-important question was a question of doctrine, and not of organization. As Prof. Fisher says, "Against the theory of the ministry, which separates the clergy as a distinct self-perpetuating body in the Church—as a close corporation—from the laity, the Reformers in all Protestant lands uttered an emphatic protest." "The purpose of the ministry was to perform acts which the flock was empowered to perform, but which from the nature of the case it must perform through agents and instruments." Had this principle been conceded by the leading Reformers in England, there never would have been any history of Puritanism. It took men many years to realize that the true question was deeper and more radical than any discussion on Church government. It was a difference of conviction as to what Christianity was. And while they were seemingly fighting about prelacy and vestments, they were really opposed to each other on the fundamental conception of religion.

A glance at the English Reformation will show what I mean. Making every allowance for the arbitrary power of masterful sovereigns and subservient parliaments and over-loyal subjects, it must be admitted that there was something besides—some spirit, some tendency, in the English Reformation that differentiated it from the movement in any Continental country. As Beard says, "The English Reformation, both in its method and result, is a thing by itself." "There was a native element stronger than any Lutheran, Calvinistic or Zwinglian influence." "It followed no precedents and was obedient only to its own law of development." And again, "One fact more than any other differentiates the English Reformation —I mean the continuity of the Anglican Church. There is no point at which it can be said, here the old Church ends, here the new begins."

That is the gist of the whole matter. The preservation of the personal, tactual connection with the Mediæval Church, and through that with the ancient Church, distinguishes the English movement. There was no popular upheaval. There was no widespread, deep disgust with the past to hurl the nation into revolution. There was no desire or attempt to substitute a doctrinal system for the ancient Constitution. On the contrary, throughout the earlier stages of the movement, doctrine was left alone and every care taken to preserve the continuity of the institution as of more importance than the doctrine. From first to last the external, visible organization of the Church was tenaciously maintained. Without any sort of hesitation, provision was made for a common prayer and ritual worship. Without the least discussion the Episcopal government was continued. There was no thought of breaking utterly with the past, and there was no man in England so forceful and dominant as either Luther in Germany or Calvin in Geneva. Instead of cutting loose from the old Church, the historical character of the Christian religion, as built up on and handed on by human lives, *i.e.*, the Catholicity of the Church in time as well as in place, was unfalteringly recognized. When the doctrinal revision came to be made, the principle of appeal to the ancient Church was unhesitatingly adopted. As Prof. Rawson Gardiner says (*History*, ii., 516), "The teaching of Laud was the teaching of

Cranmer and Hooker, viz.: that the basis of belief was the Bible, but that the Bible was to be interpreted by the tradition of the early Church." The invisible Church is not so much as mentioned in the XXXIX. Articles, and all baptized persons are declared to be members of Christ's Church. The statement in Article XX., that "the Church hath authority in matters of faith," refers undoubtedly to the whole Church and not to any portion of it, and is after all only a corollary of the fundamental principle. Beyond the historic creeds and the definitions of the four General Councils there was no disposition to define doctrine. The Articles of Religion on controverted questions are only negatively definitive. The continuity of the Church and the life of the Church were deemed of far greater importance than the elaboration of any system of theology.

Now, whether this were a right principle or not, it was the direct contradiction of the Calvinistic or Puritan theory. It was a counsel to moderation at a time when men wanted extremes, and both Puritans and Roman Catholics regarded it as treason.

English Puritanism dates from Feb. 10, 1556 (*Neale*, i., 68), with a letter written by the exiles at Geneva, in which they say, in speaking of the English Prayer Book and its provisions for worship, "We have thought fit to lay aside these human inventions and have contented ourselves with that wisdom which is found in God's Book." "We have set up such an order as in the judgment of Mr. Calvin and others is most agreeable to Scripture."

The Westminster Confession indeed uses strong language about the value and importance of the visible Church, language which Dr. Briggs has quoted with force and sympathy. But the Westminster Confession represents that later stage of Puritan conviction to which I have already referred, and cannot be taken as the expression of the original views of the Swiss Reformers. As it stands, it is careful to insist upon the true Church as being invisible, and limits the Catholicity of the visible Church as being a Catholicity of race ("not to the Jews only") and not a Catholicity in time, or historical succession. The American edition of this Confession consistently modifies the phraseology of the seventeenth century and thus more nearly approximates the Scotch platform.

The Puritans simply could not get themselves to admit that the continuation of anything in the way of discipline and worship that had obtained in the old Church would be consistent with their new-found freedom. It required great resolution and faith, no doubt, but with determined earnestness they took their stand on the text of the Bible and their own conscientious interpretation of it. And this radical difference of view crops out in every conference that was ever held in England for the sake of unity. The most superficial examination of the records of the Savoy Conference will show that compromise was simply impossible. There was no concession as to ritual or government—no concession that meant less than complete revolution of their conception of Christianity—that the Churchmen could have made, that would have been satisfactory. Baxter declared (Cardwell *Conf.*, 383) afterwards that if every concession asked for had been made, and yet if the single rubric remained asserting the salvation of infants who died immediately after Baptism, they could not conform.

I have dwelt at length upon these old disputes, because the denial of the necessity of the organic continuity of the Church—the avowed principle of Puritanism—has been the support and justification of every new Christian organization; and because I believe that if ever our unhappy divisions are to be healed we must find out the root and origin of them, and frankly and honestly express our views. For, as Carlyle says, " Only in a world of sincere men is unity possible. And there, in the long run, it is as good as certain."

I have not denounced nor condemned the Puritan position, nor have I used harsh language about the Roman position. We are all Christian men, and working for the spread of the Gospel of Christ. I have said that the Mediæval Church after Gregory VII. was a system of absolute government that emphasized the objective and external side of religion at the expense of that which was subjective and internal, encouraging the elaborate and minute definition of dogma without regard to the thought or traditions of other historical branches of the Christian Church. I have said that the principle of Continental Protestantism was, on the other hand, extremely subjective— practically a denial of the necessity of the external, organic continuity of the Christian Church, and a substitution for it of a system of doctrine based on an independent interpretation of the Bible without any necessary reference to antiquity.

I claim that neither one of these extreme positions is a complete or adequate or necessary interpretation of the spirit and purpose of the Christian Church; that each in its turn has been the occasion of lamentable divisions; and as long as they are uncompromisingly maintained there is no reasonable hope of visible unity among Christian people.

Great ideas germinate slowly at first and take root in the minds of individuals before they are accepted by the masses; and it may be so with the idea of Christian unity. It is not to be expected that religious bodies will take action until their members desire it. And again, while no scheme of unity should be considered for a moment that does not include the great historic Churches of Christendom, yet unquestionably our affinities of race and language and religion compel us to make our first appeal, not to the Greek or Roman Churches, but to that English-speaking Protestant world made up of many men of many creeds, whose forefathers were our forefathers in the English Church. And, as a matter of fact, there is an increasing number of able and earnest Christians who, though loyal Protestants, are not wedded for weal or woe to that extreme Puritan principle—nay, who are willing to modify and restate it for the sake of unity; men who believe that the conditions that evoked the heated partisanship and inordinate suspicion of the sixteenth and seventeenth centuries do not exist to-day; and who feel that in the presence of the accumulated evils of the time, no prejudice, no bitter memory of their forefathers' quarrels should stand in the way of mutual concession and fraternal sympathy. There are indeed few thoughtful men who do not regard that extreme subjective theory of religion as delusive; and no orthodox Protestant can fail to deplore the application of it which has led Dr. Martineau (*Seat of Author.*, etc., p.650) and others to the conclusion that, as the private interpretation of the Bible is the principle of Protestantism, so the authority of the Bible itself is inferior to the internal illumination, and only those Scriptures are to be retained which come up to the spiritual standard of the individual mind. As Hegel says (*Philos. of Hist.*, p. 344), "Whether a Christian doctrine stands thus and thus in the Bible is not the only question. The profoundest thought is connected with the Personality of Christ—with the historical and external." And Dr. Philip Schaff, after contrasting the outward legalism of the Mediæval Roman system with the evangelical freedom of Protestantism, says (*Apost. Ch.*, p. 678):

"Who that considers the Holy Scriptures and the idea of the One, Holy, Catholic and Apostolic Church will further venture to justify the extreme individualism, the numberless divisions and conflicting party interests into which the best positively Christian powers of Protestantism seem to be almost hopelessly rent? Who will deny that the Protestantism of this day is as much in need of reformation as was the Catholicism of the sixteenth century? This reformation we look for in the final reconciliation of Catholicism and Protestantism—in the ideal Church of the future—not a new Church, but the final, perfect product of that of the present and the past."

Thus in one form or another the old question

as to the relation between reason and authority continually recurs: whether we owe anything to the past; whether our judgments should be influenced and restrained by the definitive action of the Universal Church, or whether the interior illumination of the individual should supersede all other criteria of revealed truth. In times of revolution men may be induced in passion to denounce the imposition of any restriction upon private rights, but the permanent stability of religion, of government and of society demands the recognition of another principle. To quote Mr. Balfour: "It is true, no doubt, that we can, without any great expenditure of research, accumulate instances in which Authority has perpetuated error and retarded progress, for, unluckily, none of the influences, Reason least of all, by which the history of the race has been moulded have been productive of unmixed good. . . . Yet . . . we must not forget that it is Authority rather than Reason to which, in the main, we owe not religion only, but ethics and politics; that it is Authority which supplies us with essential elements in the premises of science; that it is Authority rather than Reason which lays deep the foundations of social life; that it is Authority rather than Reason which cements its superstructure. And though it may seem to savor of paradox, it is yet no exaggeration to say, that if we would find the quality in which we most notably excel the brute creation, we should look for it, not so much in our faculty of convincing and being convinced by the exercise of reasoning, as in our capacity for influencing and being influenced through the action of Authority" (*Foundations of Belief*, pp. 237, 238).

When, in this free Republic, the dangers that threaten our social and political fabric are felt to be the outcome in large measure of widespread irreverence for historical institutions, impatience of intellectual or moral restraint, disregard or contempt for the hopes and ideals of our forefathers, denial of the Nation as an organism with Divine sanctions, and self-assertive exploitations of visionary theories of government; surely the fashionable declamation against creeds on the part of some Christian ministers, *i.e.*, against the idea of the fixedness of any revealed truth from God, and the indiscriminate appeals to popular prejudice against reverence for the thought and practice of the Universal Church, are not calculated to restore confidence or to educate the popular mind to more sober judgment, either in politics or morals.

Dr. Schaff's candid words above quoted are a fair challenge to earnest men. Is there any adjustment possible? Is there any rational synthesis possible of private judgment and traditional authority? Are there any lines upon which we can go to work to bring about that "final, perfect product," of which he speaks, " of the Church of the present and the past"?—any middle way between tyranny and license; any fixed historic principles of the ancient Church to be maintained which shall restrain while they protect and defend the true liberty of Christian men?

This was the problem presented to the minds of the Bishops of the Protestant Episcopal Church, which they answered in the following declaration, set forth by authority of the Upper House, in the General Convention of 1886:

WHEREAS, In the year 1853, in response to a Memorial signed by many Presbyters of this Church, praying that steps might be taken to heal the unhappy divisions of Christendom, and more fully to develop the Catholic idea of the Church of Christ, the Bishops of this Church in Council assembled did appoint a Commission of Bishops empowered to confer with the several Christian Bodies in our land who were desirous of promoting godly union and concord among all who loved the Lord Jesus Christ in sincerity and truth;

AND WHEREAS, This Commission, in conformity with the terms of its appointment, did formally set forth and advocate sundry suggestions and recommendations intended to accomplish the great end in view;

AND WHEREAS, In the year 1880, the Bishops of the American Church, assembled in Council, moved by the appeals from Christians in foreign countries who were struggling to free themselves from the usurpations of the Bishop of Rome, set forth a declaration to the effect that, in virtue of the solidarity of the Catholic Episcopate, in which we have part, it was the right and duty of the Episcopates of all National Churches holding the primitive Faith and Order, and of the several Bishops of the same, to protect in the holding of that

Faith, and the recovering of that Order, those who have been wrongfully deprived of both ; and this without demanding a rigid uniformity, or the sacrifice of the national traditions of worship and discipline, or of their rightful autonomy;

AND WHEREAS, Many of the faithful in Christ Jesus among us are praying with renewed and increasing earnestness that some measures may be adopted at this time for the reunion of the sundered parts of Christendom :

NOW, THEREFORE, In pursuance of the action taken in 1853 for the healing of the divisions among Christians in our own land ; and in 1880 for the protection and encouragement of those who had withdrawn from the Roman Obedience, we, Bishops of the Protestant Episcopal Church in the United States of America, in Council assembled as Bishops in the Church of God, do hereby solemnly declare to all whom it may concern, and especially to our fellow-Christians of the different Communions in this land, who, in their several spheres, have contended for the religion of Christ:

1. Our earnest desire that the Saviour's prayer, " That we all may be one," may, in its deepest and truest sense, be speedily fulfilled ;

2. That we believe that all who have been duly baptized with water, in the name of the Father, and of the Son, and of the Holy Ghost, are members of the Holy Catholic Church;

3. That in all things of human ordering or human choice, relating to modes of worship and discipline, or to traditional customs, this Church is ready in the spirit of love and humility to forego all preferences of her own ;

4. That this Church does not seek to absorb other Communions, but rather, coöperating with them on the basis of a common Faith and Order, to discountenance schism, to heal the wounds of the Body of Christ, and to promote the charity which is the chief of Christian graces and the visible manifestation of Christ to the world ;

But, furthermore, we do hereby affirm that the Christian unity now so earnestly desired by the memorialists can be restored only by the return of all Christian communions to the principles of unity exemplified by the undivided Catholic Church during the first ages of its existence; which principles we believe to be the substantial deposit of Christian Faith and Order committed by Christ and His Apostles to the Church unto the end of the world, and therefore incapable of compromise or surrender by those who have been ordained to be its stewards and trustees for the common and equal benefit of all men.

As inherent parts of this sacred deposit, and therefore as essential to the restoration of unity among the divided branches of Christendom. we account the following, to wit:

1. The Holy Scriptures of the Old and New Testament as the revealed word of God.

2. The Nicene Creed as the sufficient statement of the Christian Faith.

3. The two Sacraments,—Baptism and the Supper of the Lord,—ministered with unfailing use of Christ's words of institution and of the elements ordained by Him.

4. The Historic Episcopate, locally adapted in the methods of its administration to the varying needs of the nations and peoples called of God into the unity of His Church.

Furthermore, Deeply grieved by the sad divisions which affect the Christian Church in our own land, we hereby declare our desire and readiness, so soon as there shall be any authorized response to this Declaration, to enter into brotherly conference with all or any Christian Bodies seeking the restoration of the organic unity of the Church, with a view to the earnest study of the conditions under which so priceless a blessing might happily be brought to pass.

I. This means, first of all, that the restored unity must rest upon an institution, as Prof. Shields says, and not upon a doctrine. There must be an honest regard for the past of the Church and an historical connection with that past. Unless we are ready to assert that the Roman and Eastern Churches are entirely outside the pale of Christendom and not included in any dream or hope of Christian unity, we are compelled to hold to this historical and objective continuity. In fact the extreme subjective view of Christianity is a denial of the idea of visible unity.

II. The Declaration means secondly that if Protestant Christians are willing to modify the extreme view of the Continental Reformers and agree to a reasonable recognition of the desirability of some organic connection with the ancient and the Mediæval Church, then the adoption of the Episcopate, in some form or another, is both the simplest and most defensible method of doing it. Without questioning the authority, or validity, or fitness of other forms of Church government, it will at least be admitted that that institution bears a different relation to the present and past of the whole of Christendom from any other ecclesiastical polity. It is simply incredible that where there is any genuine enthusiasm for Christian unity, there could be any proposition seriously entertained looking to the abandonment of the only form of organization now almost universally agreed upon in the Christian world. As there were many features in the Episcopal government of the Middle Ages that seemed to the Reformers to be incompatible with its true spiritual character; so, doubtless, to-day there are customs and precedents in the administration of the Episcopal office that we inherited from England and that are not essential to it. And so the Bishops speak of "the Episcopate locally adapted in the methods of its administration to the varying needs of nations and peoples." Doubtless, the Episcopate, in the days of Cyprian, when the average jurisdiction of a Bishop was smaller than one of our counties, was a different office in some of its external aspects from what it is to-day.

III. The regulation of the manner and matter of Public Worship is not mentioned, and no doctrinal definition of the meaning and value of the Sacraments is given, or any form, beyond the words of institution prescribed for their administration. Of course this means absolutely nothing except as an hypothesis for the sake of unity. It justifies no private experiments on the part of individual Bishops or clergy, and it involves no diminution of reverence for the teaching and Offices of the Book of Common Prayer. But even as a tentative proposition it exacts of Churchmen more of generous sacrifice both of preference and conviction than the agreement to the whole Declaration would require from any other body of Christian people.

To denounce this Declaration of the Bishops

as a sectarian effort of the Protestant Episcopal Church to absorb other Christian denominations, or to look upon the movement as anything else than unselfish, generous, and full of the spirit of Christ, is to confess to blind prejudice and real indifference to the reunion of the Christian world.

Speaking for myself, I do not look for any great and immediate results from the movement. The official responses that have been made to the Declaration so far are not specially encouraging. The largest Protestant body, numerically, in the United States, has declared that the movement for unity is both impossible and undesirable—undesirable because a variety of sects will best encourage that spirit of competition which will lead to the development of the best ideal of a Christian Church. Some of the most prominent ministers (*Question of Unity*, Bradford) in various denominations have published statements declaring that the adoption of the episcopate in any form means simply popery. One eminent divine maintains that there are no existing creeds or dogmas upon which Christians can unite, because they do not even agree in their ideas of God, and that our only hope is a communion of spiritual experience. This would satisfy Dr. Martineau.

One very able Protestant writer, while boldly contending for the recognition of the authority and the historical continuity of the visible Catholic Church, and striving vainly to reconcile it with the principles of Puritanism, dismisses Gore's statement of the Anglican position as little better than Romanism and as leaving no room for the development of the apprehension of revealed truth. It would have been fairer to take no single theologian, however high his reputation, and to judge the Anglican Church by her official utterances, which make the Catholic Creeds, the acts of the four Councils and the Book of Common Prayer her only tests of orthodoxy.

And, finally, the Declaration has been before the world for nine years and no Christian denomination has yet signified its willingness to make any concession whatever to meet the overtures of the Episcopal Church.

Is then the hope of the reunion of Christendom a mere "iridescent" or "spangled" dream? I cannot believe that. The words of our Lord and the faith of the Apostles are a standing rebuke to such scepticism. The triumphs of the early Church are a warning and a prophecy. And He who taught us to pray "Thy kingdom come" will fulfil Himself, though men doubt and fail.

> It's wiser being good than bad;
>   It's safer being meek than fierce;
> It's fitter being sane than mad;
>   My own hope is, a sun will pierce
> The thickest cloud earth ever stretched;

> That after last returns the first,
> Though a wide compass round be fetched;
> That what began best can't end worst,
> Nor what God blessed once prove accurst.

Already good has been accomplished by the action of this Church. The attention of many men has been drawn to the evil of our divisions, and Christians have been forced to declare themselves on those points which they regard as of sufficient importance to be made a bar to unity. We cannot but believe that the fair and candid examination of such grounds of difference will lead at least to an increase of brotherly charity and intelligent appreciation of one another's motives and convictions.

For us Churchmen there is every reason to thank God that one more manifest token has been given of the unique and significant place that our own Church occupies in the Christian world; and that the best spirit of the past still survives among us. Of that past we need not be ashamed. It is a story of struggle from the first for that which is wise and moderate and Catholic; for authority without tyranny; for liberty without license. Misconception and distrust have ever been the penalty that moderation pays in ages of fanaticism, and yet in the long run it is the best spirit with which to influence the world.

When the East was Arian, and when the B'shop of Rome had compromised the Faith, it was the Church in Britain to which Athanasius gave his public eulogium for its constancy to the Catholic creed. When the Roman Church was swamped with barbarian invasion and enfeebled by hopelessness and internal strife, it was Britain that furnished men—men of brain, and men of faith—to convert the Northern nations and to endure martyrdom for the cause of Christ. When Karl Magnus would found his schools and lay the basis of the University system of Europe, it was the Saxon Church of England that gave him the men of character and learning fitted for so great an enterprise. When the ancient constitutional system of the Church had been absorbed into the Ecclesiastical Monocracy of Hildebrand and Innocent, it was the English Church that fought for and won the recognition of civil and religious liberty in Magna Charta. It was an English Churchman, William of Occam, the Master of Wiclif, who taught Luther to question the validity of the Papal claims, and it was not strange that that Church which had done so much and suffered so much for the cause of constitutional freedom should become the bulwark of the Reformation. As Stubbs says (*Constitut. Hist.*, i. 267), "The English clergy in the early Norman days trained the English people for the time when the kings should court their support, and purchase their adherence by the restoration of liberties that would otherwise have been forgotten. The unity of the Church was, in the early period, the only working unity, and its liberty in the evil days that followed, the only form in which the traditions of the ancient freedom lingered. It was again to be the tie between the conquered and the conquerors, to give to the oppressed a hold on the conscience of the despot, to win new liberties and revive the old; to unite Norman and Englishman in the resistance to tyrants, and educate the growing nation for its distant destiny as the teacher and herald of freedom to all the world."

The Puritans owed to their forefathers in the Church of England whatever was right and true in their movement as an effort for freedom, just as really as did Bancroft and Laud inherit from the same mother their regard for authority and law. Whether the two theories of religion, nursed by the prejudices of ten generations, shall ever be reconciled by any corporate concession it is impossible to say. To some, perhaps to many, the unrestricted right of private judgment and individual illumination, as irreconcilable with any organic, historical continuity, or deference to the decisions and traditions of the past, will outweigh any considerations of increased power and efficiency in the work of converting the world to Christ. Yet it is an honorable distinction to this old Church of the English-speaking people; an event worthy to be reckoned with the noblest in her history—and one that her children will rejoice to remember—that, in an age of many-sided unbelief and scepticism, she was brave to forget the gloomy controversies and the bitter detractions of the past three hundred years and to send forth a message of peace and good-will to all men and women in all the world who love the Lord JESUS Christ in sincerity and keep His word.

The Holy Scriptures as the Rule and Ultimate Standard of Faith.

LECTURE II.

THE REV. CHARLES W. E. BODY, D.D., D.C.L.,
Professor of Old Testament Literature and Interpretation in the General Theological Seminary.

THE HOLY SCRIPTURES AS THE RULE AND ULTIMATE STANDARD OF FAITH.

Sanctify (or consecrate) them in the truth; thy word is truth.
—ST. JOHN xvii. 7.

FIRST amongst the articles put forth on the subject of corporate unity by the American House of Bishops at Chicago in 1886, as revised and adopted by the whole Anglo-Catholic Episcopate at Lambeth in 1888, stands the following on the Holy Scriptures: "The Holy Scriptures of the Old and New Testaments, as containing all things necessary to salvation, and as being the rule and ultimate standard of faith."

This article, with the three others which follow, according to the careful language of the collective Episcopate, "supply a basis on which approach may be by God's blessing made towards Home Reunion." A basis upon which approach to reunion may be made ; that is to say, these articles represent the fundamental elements of the Church's organic life. They contain the Catholic minima, without any one of which the full conception of the organic life of the Catholic Church can, under no circumstances, be adequately realized. They embody the germinal positions from which the other parts of Catholic faith, discipline, and practice have in all ages been nurtured and developed; and from which, therefore, when loyally and intelligently apprehended in this fundamental relationship, the numerous other important matters which corporate reunion would necessarily involve may, by God's blessing, be hopefully approached and considered. If, in the case of any religious body, the full, intelligent acceptance of any one of these positions be lacking, that religious body is not yet, in our judgment, prepared hopefully to "approach the subject of Corporate Unity" from the standpoint of historic Christianity. Hence such a body necessarily lacks the intellectual and spiritual environment required for the consideration of the further questions involved, with any hope of a successful result. In other words, the Anglican Bishops have striven to act as skilful physicians of souls in this matter. In all loving and single-hearted directness they have endeavored to concentrate the devout consideration of Christians of every name upon those fundamental positions in a defective apprehension of which the root and source of our present evils is ultimately to be found. Passing by for the time the multiform symptoms of the disease which in their external and shifting characteristics are obvious to every careful observer, they have concentrated attention upon the vital organs of the organic body of the Church's life, hidden in some one or more of which the central seat of so grave a disease must necessarily be sought. We shall do well, therefore, beloved, in this course of Lectures, to consider attentively these several fundamental articles, and, so far as we may, lovingly to invite all other Christian people to do the same, in the devout and reasonable expectation that we may all thus obtain a fuller and more living conception of the fundamental position of each in the development of the Church's corporate life; and so may, by God's blessing, perceive and correct the diseased conditions which our partial and misdirected apprehension of such fundamental matters must inevitably cause. For beyond all doubt the present divided state of our English-speaking Christianity (to go no further afield in our enquiry) does represent a diseased condition of things, and one entirely inconsistent with the ideally healthy life of the Christian Church. It is therefore the plain duty of all to track up and investigate the cause of such an unhealthy condition, so far as it exists within their own bounds. Thus used, the Chicago-Lambeth Articles may indeed prepare the way for the great blessing of visible unity which we are seeking from the hand of the Lord, from Whose hand alone it can finally come. Viewed in any other light ; not as initially fruitful and fundamental positions, from which when attained we and our brethren may together seek the guidance of the Blessed Spirit in the further consideration of whatever matters may yet remain, but as hard, mechanical conditions of reunion, which when once accepted would leave nothing further to be considered; these Articles, so far from helping on unity, may indeed be turned into a fresh barrier in the way of its speedy accomplishment.

Again and again, in conferences which have been held on this matter, it has been quite rightly urged, and that not chiefly by representatives of our own Communion, that the Church can never afford to overlook the teachings of the past Christian centuries. Certainly, no large body of Catholic Bishops, like that assembled at Lambeth in 1888, could for one moment have entertained the idea of neglecting the lessons of the well-nigh sixteen Christian centuries which intervene between us and the first promulgation of the Nicene Creed. The Chicago-Lambeth Declaration certainly means nothing of the kind. Not even from the Nicene standpoint could the Declaration be considered approximately complete, nor was it intended so to be. To say nothing of the other Sacramental Rites of the Church, which are complementary to and issue from the two great central Sacraments of the Gospel, we need recall only the great outlines which underlie all Eucharistic Offices wheresoever found—East and West and North and South—under every possible outward divergency of form and ritual, to see how momentous are the matters which lie outside the terms of the Bishops' Declaration. Looked at from the position which they themselves avow, that they are now putting forth only such matters as "supply a basis upon which approach may be, by God's blessing, hopefully made" towards full corporate unity, all is clear and plain. Complete unification presupposes a process of organic growth like that which Dr. Shields has so well portrayed in his recent most timely and valuable contribution to the subject, entitled *The United Church of the United States.* Viewed from any other standpoint than that which the Bishops themselves avow, it is hard to conceive how such a declaration could have been issued by any body of Catholic Bishops. To sum up then concisely the position for which I am contending. The loving counsel of the Bishops to all who seek for the full accomplishment of our dear Lord's purpose in the visible reunion of Christians (whether belonging to their own Communion or not) is this: In order hopefully to approach the subject, we must each and all be content to let our present positions pass, for the time being, out of sight. We must look back down the stream of Christian history till at last we find ourselves in the actual presence of the Church's still undivided organic life. Thus only can we impartially learn and consider the Divine provision by which in a sinful separatist world that unity was so long conserved and protected. This Divine provision will be found to centre in four fundamental and germinal factors. To these factors, we should give, in the first place, our fullest and undivided attention. As soon as by God's mercy we have reached a vital unity of apprehension in regard to these four fundamental factors, we may then each and all press forward with a good hope to examine from the position thus gained whatever matters may still remain—the further questions as to which there are difficulties to be solved, differences to be harmonized, deficiencies to be made good, or still richer spiritual possessions to be acquired for the doing of Christ's work in the world.

It is then from the position thus outlined that the lecturer invites your attention to-day to his allotted subject—the relation of the Holy Scriptures to the restoration of visible Church unity. We are to consider how we can best use the great fact that, thank God, the voices of Prophets and Apostles and of the Lord Himself do still sound forth in every part of our divided Christendom to enable us most efficiently to combat the evils we still deplore. Thus regarded, the subject will, I trust, approve itself as alike inviting and suggestive. A cursory examination of the literature which has from time to time appeared upon the subject of Reunion will reveal the fact that this Article of the Lambeth Declaration has, perhaps not unnaturally, at first been approached in a somewhat limited and external way. We shall find in almost every case that it has received a very inadequate treatment. Evidently to the minds of many who have written and thought upon the subject, as there was likely to be no great obstacle to the general acceptance of this Article, nothing more need be said on the matter. Clearly, however, a truer position may be found. Starting together from the momentous fact of the common general acceptance of the Holy Scriptures, how may we best use that great spiritual weapon for overthrowing the barriers which still remain in our path? Unquestionably the Divine Library of Holy Scripture was not entrusted to our care simply to be labelled "accepted" on the outside cover, but must be actively used for the healing of moral evils, whether in the individual sphere, or, as in the case before us, in the corporate life of the Church. The inquiry which is thus opened before us is of great practical moment. It will reveal a sphere for immediate and fruitful effort. It may disclose new possibilities of hope for even the smallest and most insignificant fragment of the wounded body of Christ.

A glance at the text, and at the High-Priestly prayer of our Lord for the Church from which it is taken, will sufficiently show that the view of the relation of the Holy Scriptures to organic unity above enunciated lies firmly imbedded in the fundamental teachings of Holy Writ itself. We notice that our Lord here prays, first, for the Apostles and original disciples who were the fruit of His own earthly ministry, and secondly (the transition being clearly marked at v. 20), for all the subsequent generations of Christians who shall believe on Him through the Apostolic message handed down in the Church. We note also that in each case we have a two-fold petition. Primarily, that within the sphere of the Revelation which the Lord has made, the disciples may be kept by the Father in an evil world true and faithful to their high mission, even as the Lord Himself had kept them in the days of His flesh—and then, flowing out of this primary petition, we have the prayer that, so kept, they may exhibit in the world a supernatural unity like unto the unity of the Blessed Trinity itself, to be an abiding and convincing proof of the reality of our Lord's Divine mission. Men, as they behold that unity, will instinctively recognize that a phenomenon so marvellous, a victory over the separating tendencies of the world so lasting and complete, can have its source in no mere effort of our poor sinful humanity, but is conclusive evidence of the presence in the life of regenerate men of a new and potent Divine factor, the abiding result of our Lord's mission to the world. We notice also that the connection between the primary and the resultant petition is strongly emphasized. The first is stated as the necessary foundation for the second. Only by a Divine protection, by keeping men within the fertilizing power of the Revelation already fully made, can believers go on to realize in the world the unity for which our Lord thus prays.

Hence we understand the emphatic insistence with which our Lord affirms the absolute finality of the Revelation of the Divine Nature and character which He had now, in His own Person, fully made. "I glorified thee on the earth, having accomplished the work which thou hast given me to do. . . . This is life eternal, that they should know thee the only true God, and him whom thou didst send, even Jesus Christ." Proceeding yet one step further in our Lord's thought, we see how this Revelation made in human flesh by the Eternal

Son, adequate as it is for the spiritual needs of all peoples for all time, yet becomes the actual possession of the race only through the ministry of the Apostles themselves, who are the subject of an eternal Divine election and choice. "I manifested thy name unto the men which thou gavest me out of the world: thine they were, and thou gavest them to me. . . . I have given them thy word." Further, this Divine selection of the Apostolate has already begun to fulfil its destined end. "They have kept thy word." Hence for these elect ones, the chosen repositories of this selfsame message of the Father, the Lord prays that in nothing the Revelation entrusted to their care may sustain harm or hindrance. "I pray for them, . . . for those whom thou gavest me. . . . Holy Father, keep them in thy name which thou hast given me. . . . While I was with them, I kept them in thy name which thou hast given me. . . . But now I come to thee. . . . I pray not that thou shouldest take them from the world, but that thou shouldest keep them from the evil one."

Thus divinely guarded from hurtful and antagonistic influences, the Divine message which the Apostles have themselves received in all its undimmed purity directly from the Son of God will enable them for their world-wide mission. In its power they will advance to an adequate sense and apprehension of the full meaning of their Divine vocation for the uplifting of the race. Nay, they will become partakers of the eternal mission of the Son of God Himself. Their work, like His, will be lifted far above the mere temporal circumstances of the age and environments in which it was in time accomplished. Like the great acts of the Son Himself, the Apostolic embodiment of the Divine Portraiture in the actual tongues of men becomes an eternal and undying power; a thing done in time, yet abiding unchanged for all time; a message in its essence supramundane, the true and faithful portraiture of the living message of the Father, the very Word of God, who hath Himself tabernacled amongst men. Hence we hear those wondrous words fall from the sacred lips: " They are not of the world, even as I am not of the world. Consecrate them in the truth: thy word is truth. As thou didst send me into the world, even so sent I them into the world. . . . For their sakes I consecrate myself, that they themselves also may be consecrated in truth." Further, the Divine message thus embodied in the Apostolic teaching is itself the truth—a revelation of the reality which underlies all being and all life—something entirely independent of the knowledge that man may painfully acquire for himself, either by the observance of physical sequence, or of the little world of human nature, or of the laws of human society as seen in the gradual evolution of the race. All these things may and do lead men towards the truth ; they may and do illustrate it, when it has been first received by them; they may and do modify the method of its application to their various and changing needs; but in its essence the Divine message remains always and unchangeably the same, having its foundations forever laid not in the shifting and changeful vortex of human thought and speculation, but in the eternal and changeless realities of the unveiled world of God.

Thus we come to see the full intention and purpose of this Divine treasure in the ultimate prayer which our Lord offers for its Apostolic repositories. It was to become in the Apostles themselves an effectual centre of unity, subjecting and making subservient to its fuller manifestation whatever differing types of moral character, of intellectual development, of hereditary bent or resulting environment were to be found amongst the members of the Apostolic band; uniting into one free Divine harmony the various key-notes in which were pitched the utterances of a St. Peter or a St. John, of a St. Paul or a St. James. Thus in the vital unbroken unity of the Apostolic band was laid a firm foundation for the subsequent corporate unity of the Church of all time. " Holy Father, keep them in thy name which thou hast given me, that they may be one, even as we are." No words could more emphatically reveal the heavenly, supramundane source of the unity of the original Apostolate. It was the reflection of a heavenly pattern eternally existing in the Being of God— "one as we are." It was the result of a Divine protection, in the sphere of the Revelation which the Lord had Himself brought from heaven to earth. The unity of the Church is thus a Divine and heavenly thing—a result of the ultimate manifestation of God in human flesh—"something let down into this lesser world from a higher plane of existence. Up above in the upper air is its spring and its source." The mysteries of God had been actually manifested in the facts of human life; and the result of this manifestation, as apprehended under the illumination of the Eternal Spirit, was to lift above the selfishness, mists and limitations of earth into the realization of a supreme and heavenly unity of Truth, a unity in which each several endowment and faculty of man would find at once its harmonious and its fruitful development. In the vital unity of the Apostolate, growing out of the uniqueness of the Revelation made in the Person of the Lord, built up under the overshadowing of the Holy Ghost, the Eternal Vicar of Christ on earth, was given at once the pledge and the foundation of the subsequent unity of the Catholic Church. No trace is to be found, in this fundamental teaching of our Lord Himself upon the express subject of the Church's unity, of any exclusive function of St. Peter in the matter, or of the continuance of any such function in the succession of the Bishops of Rome as the necessary guardians of the Church's unity. Here, if anywhere, in this *locus classicus* of all Scripture on the subject of unity, we should expect some declaration from our Lord on a matter so vitally momentous to all subsequent ages. Yet not only do we find no hint of such a dogma, but we have the express implication of the contrary. The message which the Eternal Son had brought to earth had become for all subsequent time the message of the whole Apostolic band. All future believers must accept it as "their message," and for all such our Lord prays that, as the natural and normal result of this acceptance, they too may be one, after the same Divine and heavenly pattern as was seen in the primal unity of the Apostles themselves. The Roman theory of mechanical unity, through the unquestioning acceptance of the decrees of an infallible successor of St. Peter, rests upon conceptions absolutely foreign to the mind of our Blessed Lord, as that mind is in this Gospel laid open before us. Of one thing we may be well assured. Whensoever in God's good time the wounds of His Church shall be healed and her corporate unity restored, that great blessing will be vouchsafed to men upon the principles here enunciated by the Supreme Bishop and Pastor of Souls. It will never be realized upon the basis of mechanical submission to a power which in its tyrannous and unlawful usurpation of functions entrusted by our Lord to the whole Apostolic college, and (so far as they could in the nature of the case be transmitted) to their successors in the collective Episcopate throughout the world, has ever been the fruitful source of discord and schisms. God hasten the day when the great Latin Patriarchate shall no longer cling to claims built up on unstable foundations of fraudulent history and wrested Scripture ; but, discarding these legacies of the past which hide from the world her true glory, may stand forth, as in ancient times, the most powerful upholder of the authority of the teaching of the collective Apostolate, the centre of world-wide Christian intercourse and fellowship, in which the Apostolic tradition is most surely and fully conserved. The Lord in His good time hasten that glorious day. The Lord bless abundantly all who in that great Communion are praying and working for that magnificent ideal. Meanwhile our own path of duty is plain and clear. In the midst of a divided Christianity, confronted still by the same yoke of Papal absolutism against which our fathers struggled, but which, alas, in these latter days wears an accentuated and emphatic form unknown in their time, it is our high vocation and privilege to proclaim as the true source of unity in the Church that message of the collective Apostolate to which our Lord here appeals. Those living authoritative voices sound forth unceasingly in the Catholic Church under the teaching of the ever-present Spirit, in the Apostolic writings of the New Testament. To the later Church, too, has been given the glory of a Divine indwelling to apply rightly the Divine fountain of Apostolic truth to the various needs of the Church's life. "The glory which thou hast given me I have given unto them" (the reference is to subsequent generations of believers) to the end that "they may be one, even as we are one; I in them, and thou in me, that they may be perfected into one; that the world may know that thou didst send me, and lovedst them, even as thou lovedst me."

The conception that the corporate unity of the Church was thus really established in the days of the Apostles themselves, and that subsequent divisions are consequently primarily due to the disregard of Apostolic authority and to declension from Apostolic teaching and example, derives much greater power and force from the results of recent historical investigation in regard to the actual character of the Apostolic age. We had been accustomed for the most part to apply to the whole period of Apostolic ministry the same picture of unbroken peace and unity which is given in the book of the Acts, of the early days of the Church of Jerusalem, when the glory of the first manifestation of the Spirit tabernacling in the Body of the Lord was yet undimmed. But the critical investigation of the last half-century (much of it at the time hostile, exaggerated, and distorted) has in its final outcome given us a vivid portraiture of the Apostolic founders of the Church far more Scriptural, far more true to fact and to history, than this idyllic dream of our earlier fancy. To quote from one of the greatest living teachers of our Communion : "As we now study the Apostolic records afresh," he says, " we see those master-builders at their work. No easy, heaven-born task this of theirs. Things do not slide into their places, nor come together at a rapid word. No, we see these men toiling as we might toil, doubting as we doubt, jarring as we jar; stumbling, hesitating, disheartened, distressed, beaten, baffled, yet still laboring, still carried through, still moving towards the goal. . . . The Church of Christ . . . did not start up as in a night like some magical palace, without the sound of saw or axe or hammer. Nay, indeed, the noise of the stone-yard is busy about us as this temple of God is raised course by course. With effort, with struggle, under pressure, in hot argument, in anxious uncertainty, in dreary disappointment, in weary delays, in crucial agonies, stone is laid to stone, and beam to beam. The victory of the Spirit proves its mastery, not by selecting its own conditions, but by achieving its aims through the conditions made for it in human history." Read your Acts and Epistles again in the light of such a book as Dr. Hort's *Judaistic Christianity*, the work of perhaps the greatest authority on this special subject in Christendom—one but the other day removed from us by death—and you will see that this picture is in no way overdrawn.

The history of the Apostolic age depicts the accomplishment of the unification of the Church in spite of obstacles far greater than any which can ever again confront her, and in the face of barriers which stretched back into an immemorial past, and claimed with real though partial truth the sanction of an actual Divine institution. The problem before the Apostolic age was not, as now, to reunite Christians severed by differences comparatively recent and secondary in their nature, deriving all their unhappy force from mere human insistence and the prescription of, at the most, a few centuries. The task before the Apostles was a far different one. Theirs it was to create a united Christendom out of elements the most discordant, severed by barriers and animosities of age-long duration. They struggled to unite in a vital harmony of polity, thought, and action, the Jewish Christians who continued to enforce the painful physical rite of circumcision upon their own race (a large section of whom desired to make this compulsory upon all Christians, whether of Jewish descent or not), and the converts from the heathen peoples with their various and differing racial characteristics, diversities of thought, language, and customs, all alike fundamentally severed from the Jews by an age-long preparation for the Gospel peculiar to themselves, of a kind absolutely alien, foreign and incomprehensible to God's ancient people. The task, moreover, was almost indefinitely complicated by the existence of a world-wide Jewish dispersion, which brought the two conflicting elements into close juxtaposition in whatever place a church was founded, and gave scope for abundant dissension and misrepresentation in every Christian centre. How great was the agony of the tension that St. Paul endured in his life-long conflict for the unity of the Church on the one side, and for the Catholicity which insured to the heathen Christians an equal position with the Jews in the Church of God on the other, we can read between the lines of his Epistles. The point I wish now to emphasize is, that this creation of a united Catholic Church in spite of such stupendous obstacles was the common work of all the Apostles, energized by the power of a common faith, inspired by one and the same Eternal Spirit. It was not brought about by conciliar decrees merely, for nothing is more clear than that the Apostolic decision at Jerusalem was relative strictly to but one special crisis of the history, and, save in the spirit it expressed, had but little directly to do with the subsequent course of events. The conciliatory spirit of a St. James; the spiritual discernment of a St. Peter, quickened as it had been at the outset by special supernatural enlightenment in the matter of the Gentile Cornelius; the deep grasp of the meaning of our Lord's Work and Person in its relation to this special matter possessed by St. Paul, coupled as it was in his case with an almost boundless affection for his countrymen after the flesh; these and such as these were the factors which preserved the vital unity of the Apostolate itself under the terrible strain to which that unity was then exposed, and so made this very unity efficacious throughout the length and breadth of the Roman world for building up a homogeneous and harmonious Christendom. In that first unique period of little more than a quarter of a century which witnessed the creation and consolidation of a Catholic Church, victorious over all barriers of privilege, race, heredity, wealth, power, custom, and environment, the great High-Priestly prayer of the Son of God received its unique fulfilment, a fulfilment the significance of which can never be exhausted.

The vital unity of the Apostolate, which had its root in the power of the common faith, approved itself as superior to every opposing influence which could be massed against it. The unity of the Apostolate became the source and the strength of the corresponding supernatural unity of the Catholic Church.

The more vividly then that we realize the real splendor of that first typical victory of the unity of the kingdom of God over all separating barriers, the better shall we understand the power of the authoritative message of the united Apostolate to conserve the unity thus initially won. Now as ever the Church is built upon the foundation of the Apostles and Prophets. The voices of the Prophets heralding the coming kingdom, interpreting for us the lessons of the ancient preparatory dispensation, were ratified and gathered up into a living unity in the Person and Work of the Lord. The voice of the Lord sounds forth in the Church in the message of the united Apostolate. Age by age the Church sits as a learner at the feet of this band of authoritative teachers, whose living oracles are still efficient for the dissolving of each separating tendency which threatens to mar the Divine unity of the Body of Christ. The authority of the Apostolate, ministered through their living words and deeds, yet growing ever stronger and more dear through the adhesion of each successive Christian age, should have been adequate to conserve the Church's unity. Now that, owing to a partial disregard of that authority, this unity has been so grievously marred in its outward and corporate manifestation, to no other source can we go that is competent to restore the ancient desolations of the supernatural structure. The words of the great African Father, St. Augustine of Hippo, uttered fourteen centuries ago in reference to the powerful Puritan separatists of his own day, are equally true and equally suggestive in our present difficulties. In this conflict "nothing conquers but the truth; the victory of truth is love." Or again, "Why, brethren, is it that we find it so difficult to be at one? Because men contend from the earthly standpoint, because they will to be but earth, earthy." For this the great teacher can see but one remedy: "Let us, therefore, lift up our eyes to Him who cannot err. Let Him teach us what the Church is." Contrast with this the portraiture of the great leader of the Donatists or Separatist party, as it is summed up by a German scholar in a monograph of recognized authority on the subject: "Parmenian," says Ribbeck, "like all Separatists, lays stress on the letter rather than the spirit of Holy Scripture. Hence he attached greater importance to external than to internal marks of separation between the Church and the world." In a word, the conception of the living authority of the Apostolic message as such had been lost. It had been replaced by that of the mere mechanical authority of isolated expressions of an inspired document. To the testimony of St. Augustine, already cited, we may add that of another Latin Father, one of the greatest Bishops who ever sat in the chair of St. Peter. Leo I., Bishop of Rome, writing to Flavian, Patriarch of Constantinople, on an ever memorable occasion, says: " The source of error is, that, when men are hindered by some obscurity, they run not to Prophets, or Apostles, or Evangelists [mark the phraseology], but to themselves. Hence they continue to be teachers of error because they have not been disciples of the truth."

The time has now come, thank God, when at least we Anglican Christians can look back at the history of the past alike with adequate historical knowledge and sufficient impartiality to enable us to trace at least the outlines of the process by which the Church's hold upon the living Apostolic message became sufficiently slack to give to the forces of disunion their opportunity of partial triumph. Read any of the great Fathers of the early centuries. Take, for example, St. Irenæus in the second century, St. Athanasius in the fourth century, St. Leo of Rome in the fifth, men who were the most conspicuous examples of defenders of the faith and unity of the Church, and you will be struck by the constantly recurring evidence of the extent to which the authority of the Apostolate, as shown in their words and their work, was to them an abiding, present force. Gradually as the centuries rolled by and the age of the Apostles receded into the dim past of history, whilst great teachers had been raised up in brilliant succession to defend the Faith against the perils of those later times, the authority of these teachers began to dim in some measure that of the Apostles of the Lord.

The evil was much aggravated by the growing habit of pressing to an altogether exorbitant extent the dominant allegorical method of interpretation of Holy Scripture. This method, rooted as it is in the true principle that every passage of Holy Scripture receives its most fruitful interpretation when viewed in the light of the deepest teachings of the whole Revelation, yet by its illegitimate exaggeration went far to altogether hide the message of the separate parts of Scripture under a luxuriant growth of the pious meditations of devout minds. One can readily see how under this treatment individual souls might gain much spiritual profit, whilst the wider lessons of Holy Writ which deal with the perils of the Church's corporate life would be largely obscured. In this way it became possible that in a rude age, when the very foundations of Western civilization were being slowly and painfully relaid amongst the dominant Teutonic peoples, the false witness of the Decretals was able to gain acceptance and give the lie to the plainest teachings of the Apostolic history. Thus was the Papacy impelled forwards on that path of ecclesiastical despotism which was mainly responsible for the first great schism between East and West.

A little later, as the West pursues its now isolated course, we find a growing tendency to discourage amongst the lay-people the reading of the Holy Scriptures, whilst the vast multiplicity of the Patristic writings necessitated an attempt to correlate and harmonize them in some more compendious form. This natural tendency synchronized with the period of rising influence of the Aristotelian philosophy, introduced into Western Europe through the Arab conquests. The combined result was seen in the position gained by the *Sentences* of Peter Lombard and the *Summa* of St. Thomas, with the mass of scholastic literature to which these great works gave birth. The work of the great scholastic Doctors was undoubtedly from many points of view of great and abiding value. Their desire on the one side to harmonize and make effectual the spiritual inheritance of the past contained in the writings of the Fathers, and on the other to interpret the unchanging Faith afresh to a new age so as to meet the needs of men trained by new instruments of human thought, was lofty and true. But it must still be confessed that the indirect influence of the diversion of the thought and spirituality of centuries so exclusively into these channels was most mischievous, and accentuated the growing disregard of the Apostolic message itself. The *Summa* and the *Sentences* practically replaced the "Apostles and Prophets" as the living fountains of the Church's thought and guidance. Not all the influence of a Nicholas de Lyra or a Wyclif could greatly avail to stem the rising tide. For another century the decay of Scriptural study and influence continued unchecked. Hence, when the invention of printing struck off the shackles from literature, and the diffusion of Greek learning consequent upon the fall of the Eastern Empire rendered possible the study of the Apostolic writings and of the great Greek theologians in their original tongue, the rebound was startling in its intensity, and almost necessarily one-sided and disproportioned in its results. Men had lost the knowledge of the right use of the great spiritual weapon thus suddenly placed in their hands. They had to recover slowly through the discipline of stormy centuries that full conception of the office of Holy Scripture which had been instinctive in the Apostolic churches of earlier days.

The evil was aggravated by many concurrent mischiefs. The abuses and corruptions of the Church discredited its ancient polity and organization. The recognized Papal pretensions fatally confounded the authority of the Divinely constituted body of the Episcopate with the radically antagonistic claim of the Papacy to sum up all ecclesiastical authority in itself. It must be confessed that the attitude of a large part of the Episcopate was strangely unsympathetic in this supreme crisis, and rather aggravated than diminished the strain. Moreover, the religious leaders of the New Learning themselves, so far, at least, as they were represented by men like John Calvin or Martin Chemnitz, brought to the study of Holy Scripture minds fashioned in the current scholastic dialectics, the influence of which they were unable to shake off. The Holy Scriptures were thus too exclusively regarded as a fountain of doctrine. The intellectual and philosophical aspects of the Divine message obtained undue predominance over its moral and institutional sides. The balanced language of the English Bishops in their authoritative declaration of 1543, entitled *A Necessary Doctrine*, etc., soon ceased to reflect the dominant temper of the Continental Reformers. These words of our spiritual fathers, thank God, are far more likely to be heeded now, and I therefore give a short extract from them: "The unity of the Catholic Church [say they], which all Christian men (in the Apostles' Creed) do profess, is conserved and kept by the help and assistance of the Holy Spirit of God in retaining and maintaining of such doctrine and profession of Christian faith and true observance of the same as is taught by the Scripture and doctrine Apostolic, and particular churches [the context shows that the reference is to the existing historic churches of Europe] ought not, in the said doctrine so accepted and allowed, to vary, one from another, for any mere arrogance or any other worldly affection, but inviolably to observe the same, so that by reason of that doctrine each church that teacheth the same may be worthily called (as it is indeed) an Apostolic church, that is to say, following such teaching as the Apostles preached, with ministration of such sacraments as be approved by the same." These men, it is clear, regarded the Apostolic Scriptures as a living rule and standard by which the deposit of faith handed down in the organic Church was in every age to be tried, conserved and enriched.

On the Continent this view was almost everywhere being replaced by a conception of the office of Holy Scripture which divorced it entirely from the historic Church, making it a storehouse of doctrinal propositions, from which the true faith was to be afresh selected and gathered. The

Holy Scriptures ceased to be the living continuous representatives of Apostolic authority, witnessing to the Divine and binding character of Apostolical institutions and actions as well as of Apostolical teachings and words. They were interpreted, not in the light of the actual faith of the Apostolic churches, as the same had been continuously handed down through the long ages of the Church's warfare, but with a growing disregard of historical continuity, according to the bent and fancy of great individual teachers. Those were times in which, owing to the lack of our modern facilities for historical research, and the discredit into which the appeal to history had been thrown by the forged Decretals and the abuse of Patristic authority, men were far less able than now to trust the historical continuity of Christian doctrine as a witness to the right use of the Apostolic Scriptures. Hence it is no wonder that Confessions of differing types grew and multiplied. The divisions of Protestantism became a by-word and a scandal, which largely gave strength to the counter-revolution of the Roman Church, and discredited its cause in the minds of thinking, devout men. The battles of the Confessions created as much bitterness and monopolized as much attention as any scholastic controversies of mediæval times. Meanwhile the Roman Church looked on with contempt at the rapid evolution of dissensions, disintegration, and division, and was strengthened the more in its own exclusive claims. Nor should an Anglican Priest be slow to confess how the English Church, torn and vexed by doctrinal controversies imported from abroad, vainly sought relief by undue dependence upon the civil power; how in consequence the germs of fresh dissensions were quickened into active life; how a largely dominant but thoroughly unscriptural Erastianism, particularly under the early Hanoverian monarchs, with their unconstitutional despotism in matters affecting the Church, weakened her spiritual power and thus distorted and disguised her real beauty in the eyes of Christian people. Such causes largely accelerated (though they certainly did not justify) the greatest secession we have ever suffered, in the separation of the Methodist body, nurtured, be it remembered, from infancy to far-developed youth within the Communion of the Mother Church.

So far, then, we have passed in rapid review the sad record of causes which lie at the back of the present deplorably divided state of American Christianity. For be it remembered that almost the only purely American contribution to the cause of sectarianism has been merely to subdivide in comparatively unimportant and unessential particulars the systems inherited from the Old World. Only one really large or important religious body amongst us claims an exclusively American origin. It is noticeable that that body, "The Disciples of Christ," itself exists as a protest against division. It aims, albeit in a quite mistaken way, to bring about the union of Christians by forming one more denomination for the purpose, and by discarding not only all Confessions but all Creeds. The obstacles to corporate unity are thus much less than they might have been had the separating spirit received some powerful native and American embodiment.

The foregoing historical retrospect will have been faulty indeed if it has not shown how largely the loss of corporate unity has sprung from the neglect or misapprehension of the office of the Apostolic Scriptures. Yet all the while those precious Apostolic fountains of the Church's life were lying ready to hand, able when rightly used to minister that spirit of unity which would have vanquished every Separatist tendency. In the emphasis which they lay upon the true source of authority in the Church, through the living permanence of the whole Apostolic foundation, whether institutional or doctrinal; in their historical breadth and sweep, carrying men's minds away from local or racial or mere passing questions which at any particular age may acquire undue predominance, to those Divine pictures of long ago, in which amidst all their differing forms the unchanging perils of the Church and of humanity are typically portrayed and met; in the lessons of patience we learn as we watch the foundations of the Kingdom of God slowly and gradually prepared and laid through the long centuries of time covered by the Biblical narrative; in the vital reciprocal connection which they reveal between Christian doctrine and Christian life in all its forms, whether individual or corporate ; above all, in the vision which they give of the one Person of the Incarnate Lord as the root and centre of both the Church's life and the Church's faith ; the Apostolic writings contain within themselves the necessary spiritual bond of unity alike for the institutional and the dogmatic life of the Church. Nor are there wanting many signs that the reverent devotion with which Christians everywhere in our days are turning from their own preconceived ways to sit humbly and intelligently at the feet of the great Apostolic teachers is already playing a most important part in preparing the way for corporate reunion. In whatever measure it be true, as a distinguished American thinker has said, that "the centrifugal period of Protestantism is over, the centripetal period has begun," the moving cause is in the main a deeper appreciation and more intelligent apprehension of the fulness of the Apostolic message. Men have begun to catch sight of a more glorious vision than they knew before.

They have recognized the possibility of reproducing in the world Apostolic unity as the Apostles themselves portrayed and fashioned it. We have seen in our day the upgrowth of a school of Biblical interpretation at once historical, scholarly, and reverent, which has quickened in every part the spiritual force of the Anglican Communion, by teaching us to see in the historic personality and work of the Apostles themselves an integral part of the whole Revelation. We have watched the rise of theologians outside our own Communion, of men like Dr. Milligan in Scotland and Dr Dale of Birmingham, whose writings on leading doctrines of the Faith have been welcomed everywhere amongst English-speaking Christians as thoroughly Catholic and Scriptural, powerful to the breaking down of doctrinal differences and to their solution in a deeper and truer unity. In the great Roman Communion we have seen the Supreme Pontiff reversing the dominant practice if not the theoretical rule of his Communion for centuries past, and enforcing the duty of the deeper study of Holy Scripture as the real remedy for the evils of our time. That Allocution has already borne manifest and widespread results. Within the last few weeks the following advice was formally given by Cardinal Gibbons to candidates for Confirmation in the capital city of America as reprinted in the *Washington Post:* "My children,

I want to impress upon you one thing which I have no doubt will be a surprise to some. I want each and every one of you to procure a Bible. I exhort you to read the Word of God with reverence and devotion. Read the Holy Scriptures diligently. This is an admonition to you of the Church of God, delivered by the prelate of God in the Church." No wonder that with such forces at work we have the following testimony from a leading English Nonconformist minister : " The increasing gravitation of Christian churches towards each other is indisputable. We cannot help it. The psychological climate created by the ministry of the Spirit of God in these later years renders it impossible for us to be content with our traditional separations, and satisfied with our human and mischievous sectarianisms."

True, as of old, when the Apostle discerned a great door and effectual opened before him, there are many adversaries. None, perhaps, amongst the discouraging signs is more terribly alarming than the growing famine of an intelligent knowledge of the Word of God which our sad divisions have directly produced, by practically banishing from our entire educational curriculum the real study of that Divine Library and of that body of Divine Truth, which is above all other things most efficacious alike for expanding the human mind or moulding the character of our youth. I would that the day may soon come which may find the Protestant Episcopal Church furnished with a great central University, adequately equipped and endowed to exert its full influence upon the education and thought of our country; where, as in the Universities of the Old Land, the ideals of our fathers of the English Reformation may be realized, and the place of Biblical and Sacred study in the plan of a Christian University more effectually vindicated before the intelligent people of this great country than has yet been the case.

Beyond all doubt, and the thought is gladly emphasized by many outside the pale of our Communion, the American Church has an unique and glorious office to perform in the building up of a united American Christianity. It behooves us, then, clergy, and especially laymen, to see to it that the means are forthcoming, and that speedily, which will give to this Church of the Reconciliation the same measure of influence in the smaller towns and amongst the more scattered populations of this country that she already possesses in the larger centres of population. When thoughtful and devout minds are looking with hope and affection to this Church as especially entrusted with the cause of corporate unity; when God by His providence is summoning us to gird ourselves for so mighty a vocation, how inexpressibly culpable will be our sluggishness or apathy in claiming for our Church that measure of influence throughout the length and breadth of the land to which she is clearly and indisputably entitled.

Let us, then, beloved, do our part hopefully and lovingly in this, as yet, day of small things, believing that beneath all the turmoil and the discord of our divided Christianity are being laid slowly and firmly, by a Divine Hand, the foundations of what has been so well termed a "United Church of the United States," which shall yet exercise a healing and benign influence throughout our land; a Church holding firmly amid all secondary differences to the fulness of the Apostolic message, and solidly compacted together by the conserving bond of Apostolic organization and worship.

> God's Spirit in the Church
>   Still lives unspent, untired,
> Inspiring hearts that fain would search
>   The truths Himself inspired.
> Move, Holy Ghost, with might
>   Amongst us as of old,
> Dispel the falsehood and unite
>   In true faith the true fold. Amen! Amen!

The Two Creeds.

LECTURE III.

VEN. CHARLES S. OLMSTED,

OF COOPERSTOWN, N. Y.

Archdeacon of the Susquehanna.

THE TWO CREEDS.

THE best method by which to arrive at a definition of the Creeds, and at the same time to discover what they involve, and what relation they bear to other doctrinal standards and to the reunion of Christendom, is to trace their origin and history.

I.

It will not be denied that the entire idea, fact and doctrine of Christianity may be reduced in the last analysis to a single concept, viz., that God is become Man in the Person of Jesus Christ.

Tertullian said, "The consciousness of God is the original dowry of the soul." This consciousness is the most patent and pervasive fact in human history. It enters into the very fibre of all human life. To it the Ethnic religions owe their being and vitality. The world has always desired

God as an object of worship and as an object of knowledge. Even more, it has ever desired to be united to God. However distorted the notion of how such an union may be effected, in the fugitive incarnations of Indian culture, or in the apotheoses of Hellenic thought, it proclaims the dim but persistent hope which is native to the human heart.

In the great mystery of our Christian faith we find how man can be united to the Absolute and Abiding Reality which underlies the universe. God answers man's hope by taking manhood into God. In a manner undreamed of by human religions the desire of those religions is accomplished. In a manner due to Divine wisdom alone the union is effected. The Son of God assumes our nature into His Divine Person. It is not by changing Himself into man, nor by uniting entirely to Himself a human person, nor by exalting a single man on account of his goodness to become God, nor by uniting all men in their persons to the nature of God that the Son of God unites God and man.

The Incarnation takes place in a Divine manner, undreamed of by the world, and is proved not only by its fitness to the desire and need of man, but by its Divine method of becoming. The nature of man is united to the nature of God in the Person of the Eternal Son.

The true knowledge of the Incarnate Son of God is the peculiar possession of Christians. He Himself revealed it to certain men whom He named Apostles. He lived with them, and permitted them to see and hear the word of life. They paid to Him Divine worship. They acknowledged Him to be the Lord. They knew Whom they believed, for they had an unction from the Holy One. They spent their lives in His service. They poured out their blood in witness to the truth of His Divinity.

In subsequent ages the Apostolic witness was felt to be true by vast multitudes of people, who gave themselves to the Lord. They lived the life of Christ. They entered here on an heavenly state of being. They fed on immortal food. They contemplated in simple faith the condescension of their Master, Who, that He might "better the quality and advance the condition" of their nature had come down from Heaven and was made flesh and had humbled Himself yet more, even to the death of the Cross. They knew the witness of the Holy Spirit with their spirit. They knew the Father, knowing the Son. They had entered the Kingdom of Christ through the door of grace and pardon. They looked for the likeness of their Risen Lord not only in the spiritual part of their nature, but also in their bodies, and they rejoiced in the hope that was laid up for them in Heaven.

From the day of Pentecost Christians were familiar with certain facts of revelation which Christ had come into the world to bring. They had a body of doctrine, which they had received, not having chosen it, or any portion of it, for themselves. The Lord had said to the Apostles, "Ye believe in God, believe also in me." He had spoken to them of the Comforter and of the things pertaining to His Kingdom. He had directed them to make disciples of all nations by baptizing them into the Name of the Father and of the Son and of the Holy Ghost. He had thus outlined those summaries of belief which afterward were used in the Church on the admission of new members to the Baptismal privilege, all substantially alike, all containing some mention of the chief facts in Christ's redemptive work, and of the ineffable mystery of the Trinity. The chief creed of the West, called the Apostles', which it is believed can be traced, very nearly as we have it, to the middle of the second century, embodies them all, and in fact embodies that which they stood for --the universal tradition of the Church of the Apostles.

But into the ever-widening circle of the Catholic Church great nations came, and under the shadow of its precious tree sat down to rest. Sages from the East and from the South were attracted by its marvellous light. It could not be long ere the simplicity of the faith would be exposed to the influence of strange and intricate philosophies. Here and there the effete ineptitudes of an earlier time engrafted themselves upon the pure root of truth and flourished with renewed vigor. "While there were no heretics, there was no need to guard against heresy,"* but now it was no longer possible for the Church simply to live her belief. She must learn to discover its significance. That which she had so deeply felt must be intellectually more and more interrogated and explained.

Converted philosophers were forward to construe the person of Jesus Christ according to the formulas of Chaldaic Judaism or of heathen schools, and we are sufficiently familiar with Ebionism and Docetism, and the host of errors that followed for centuries in the wake first of the one and then of the other.

The question, humanly speaking, was, could the Church keep her peculiar treasure, which she had contemplated in her simple and believing heart far more than she had meditated with her reason? If so, she must not forbear to treat it as an object of intellectual inquiry, much as she would shrink from subjecting the nature of her adorable Head to human questions and reasonings. She had a true and unchangeable belief in

---

* Burton's *Ecclesiastical History*, p. 404.

the Son of God and the Father Whom He came to reveal, but under the repeated attacks of rationalistic denial not all her teachers at all times could give adequate statements in scientific language concerning it. She had a delicate spiritual tact, which always prompted her to perceive the incipiency of error, but she could not always meet it at once in words of unquestioned clearness and with concurrent authority. She was like a child who is told that its God is the rocks and woods and waters. It knows what it worships, and that its God is not the rocks and woods and waters, but it is at a loss to describe this article of its belief in impregnable terms.

Melancholy as the primitive heresies were, they compelled the Church to direct her reason upon the all-absorbing theme; they compelled believers to become theologians; they compelled the Church in its collective capacity to formulate definitions of faith.

In the face of those Christological heresies, the Church for five whole ages had to gather what had been handed down from the first by her universal tradition concerning the Only-Begotten; she had to translate the language of the spiritual world into that of the intellectual; she had to exhibit Divine realities as best she might in the foreign medium of human speech; she had to reduce the varieties of theological terms and statements to technicality, and purge them of any supposed perverse connotations, lifting the term homoöusion, for instance, out of all Gnostic, Manichean and Sabellian senses, to which it had been appropriated, and so authoritatively to establish an exact scientific terminology, by which the relations of the Three Subsistences eternally interior to the Substance of the Godhead might be for ever guarded from misapprehension.

As the Apostles' Creed had embodied the tradition of the Church, the Creed called the Nicene scientifically stated that tradition. Ante-Nicene theology did not differ in essence at all from the theology of Athanasius and Nice, of Cyril and Ephesus, of Leo and Chalcedon, of Sophronius and that Council of Constantinople in which the influence of his unforgotten faith determined matters. It had simply used terms in an unscientific manner, terms often good enough in themselves, but not always taken to mean the same thing by different minds.

That Creed which is called the Nicene, which is really no doubt an old Palestinian Creed adopted with variations at Nice and afterward at Constantinople, with additions, and expressly confirmed by the authority of the Ephesine and Chalcedonian Councils and now used by us with certain differences, contains the substance of all earlier summaries of the faith very much as the

Epistles of the New Testament contain the substance of the Gospels. It is dogmatic truth, *i.e.*, revealed beliefs subjected to processes of thought, analyzed, harmoniously viewed, consolidated, measured in the light of concurrent and traditional conviction, authorized by the Church representatively, accepted without qualification by the Church universally, of perpetual obligation even in its minutest points upon all portions of the Christian world. It crystallized Apostolic and universal tradition. It set forth in as few words as possible the great body of Divine faith which Our Blessed Lord gave into His Church's hands at the beginning, and which had been proved all along by the Scriptures. It juridically expressed the Church's ecumenical mind. It stated systematically what had been unsystematically diffused through the writings of an innumerable throng of witnesses. It embalmed the spirit of essential truth. It was the chorus of fathers, liturgies, those "acted creeds," as they have been finely called, councils, summaries of belief. It was like the cloud which gathering and deepening mists from every quarter of the summer sky have formed, which sustains the light of the sunrising, and glows in the splendors of the passing day. Looked at in their bare outline the Creeds may seem like Grecian temples, severe and straight on every side; but surrounded by the piety and virtue of the lives that have lived them, and illumined by the One Supreme and spotless life to which they testify, they soar like Gothic minsters, with lines lost in lines till the whole is softened into a vision of imperishable beauty.

As the Church is not an organ of continuous revelations, but the repository of the faith once delivered to the saints, so she is not the Author but only the Editor of her Creeds. He who gave her the deposit of the faith, gave her ability to define and defend it. She cannot make that to be truth which was not truth from the beginning. She cannot make discoveries of things to be believed in order to salvation in the fourth or in the nineteenth century, which were not proposed to the faith of Christians in the first or in the second. Speaking as a whole, she is no more liable to error in one age than in another. She is not a school of development in which philosophical fancies, called pious opinions, though often impious, may be exalted to the rank of dogma. Could she assemble her sons from every quarter to-day in a lawful General Council, they could in no wise change or rescind the Creeds of the Ecumenical Councils. They could only declare their unfeigned assent and continued allegiance to every article contained in them.

Mr. Illingworth in his Bampton Lectures says, "The various heresies which attempted to make the Incarnation more intelligible, in reality explained it away: while council after council, though freely adopting new phraseology and new conceptions, never claimed to do more than give explicit expression to what the Church from the beginning had implicitly believed. . . . Christian theology arose like all other human thought, in meditation upon a fact of experience—the life and teaching of Jesus Christ, and having arisen, reacted, also like other human thought, upon the fact which it explained, illuminating, intensifying, realizing the significance of the fact."*

We find then that the Creed, called the Nicene, embodies the intellectual result of a long and continuous profession of the great facts of Divine revelation. It stands to the Apostles' Creed in the relation in which St. Augustine said the New Testament stands to the Old. The Nicene Creed is latent in the Apostles', and the Apostles' Creed is patent in the Nicene. The Nicene Creed reflects the intellect, while the Apostles' Creed reflects the heart of the primitive Church. The Nicene Creed contains the matured reflection of theologians, the Apostles' Creed contains the simple facts on which believers fed.

When questioned as to their faith, Catholics could say the Apostles', and when cross-ques-

---

* *Personality, Human and Divine*, p. 11.

tioned they could say the Nicene. The one is not diverse from the other. In its substance it contains nothing in excess of the other. The Nicene Creed is simply the amplified statement of the articles of faith handed down from the days of the Apostles. It is the Apostles' Creed subjectively viewed, not altered. It is not that or any other old formula made over to suit a philosophy of foreign imposition. It is simply the subject enlarged in itself. "These Catholic declarations of our belief," says Hooker, "delivered by them which were so much nearer than we are unto the first publication thereof, and continually needful for all men at all times to know, these confessions as testimonies of our continuance in the same faith to the present day, we rather use than any other gloss or paraphrase devised by ourselves, which, though it were to the same effect, notwithstanding could not be of the like authority and credit." *

II.

The Creeds involve the existence and use of Apostolic tradition, through the whole body of which its vital diffusion can be traced by the dogmatic historian. The Anglican Church teaches that "Holy Scripture containeth all things necessary to salvation: so that whatever is not read

---

* *Works*, Church's Keble Ed., vol. ii., p. 182.

therein, nor may be proved thereby, is not to be required of any man, that it should be believed as an article of the Faith, or be thought requisite or necessary to salvation."*

The candid and learned Du Pin agreed to this very principle, and said in his *Commonitorium*, now lost: "This we (*i.e.*, Gallicans) will gladly admit, provided that tradition be not excluded, which does not exhibit new articles of faith, but confirms and explains those things which are contained in Holy Scripture, and fences them by new safeguards against those who are otherwise minded, so that nothing new is said, but only the old in a new way." † Would that all Roman theologians were as wise and moderate in their estimate of the right office and nature of tradition! The Creeds and that tradition which they represent add nothing to Holy Scripture any more than an image reflected in a mirror adds to the weight of the mirror. They were never felt by the whole Church to be fountains of the faith. They were always felt to be symbols of it, outlines of it, plain guides to it, which the faithful were to fill out and follow when Scripturally informed and sacramentally animated. As the Holy Eucharist sets forth, exhibits, pleads, applies, the Sacrifice of our Lord on Calvary, but adds nothing to its

---

* Art. VI. of Religion.
† See Pusey's *Eirenicon*, p. 213.

merit, so the Creeds add nothing to the substance of Holy Scripture. They keep us from misunderstanding its general drift; they apply to it a consistent interpretation. The Eucharist does not add to the efficacy of the Cross, but gives its efficiency, and the Creeds, in like manner, though revealing nothing new, give clearness to that which is revealed once for all. They do not enter into the interpretation of particular texts of Holy Scripture, but they form the result of what might be termed a higher criticism of all Scripture. They are the classics of doctrinal literature, Homeric in their dignity, not because we cannot in any degree read between their lines the history of their scientific expression, nor weigh some of their statements in the scales of contemporaneity, but because they are, through their universal acceptance, lifted above the merely historic atmosphere. They are touched with a heavenly light. They have rather the unwrinkled grandeur of statues than the charactered coloring of pictures. We value them as being not only primitive, but universal; the Church, having spoken once on the subjects contained in them, having, in the nature of things, spoken for all time. They are removed above the stress of any individualistic or provincial thought. They have attained, not to old age but to agelessness. They have in them that immortal quality which invests the whole machinery and operation of God's work in the world. In a word, and in every sense of the word, they are Catholic.

The Creeds are the most clearly ascertained tradition of the primitive ages; and it is a happy circumstance that this is so, because on the field of doctrine they subtend a larger angle of interpretation than any other document of ancient or of modern times. In the matters of chief concern to us as Christians, the Trinity, the Incarnation, the Atoning work of Christ, the agency of the Holy Spirit in the means of grace and the life to come—they set forth the very spirit of Divine truth, and "it is not likely," as has been well said by Waterland, "that any whole Church of those times should vary from Apostolic doctrine in things of moment, but it is, morally speaking, absurd to imagine that all the churches should combine in the same error and conspire to corrupt the doctrine of Christ."*

"No man," said Bishop Bull, "can oppose Catholic consent, but he will at last be found to oppose both the Divine oracles and sound reason." Bishop Ridley, in the *Necessary Doctrine of a Christian Man*, said that "All those things which were taught by the Apostles, and have been by the whole universal consent of the Church of Christ

---

* Waterland's *Works*, vol. iii., p. 611.

ever since that time taught continually and taken always for true, ought to be received, accepted and kept as a perfect doctrine Apostolic."

Keble, in speaking of St. Athanasius as the one preëminent among divines, ancient or modern, who had committed his cause to the witness of Scripture, says, " But the more unfeignedly he revered the Bible, the more thankfully did he avail himself of the greatest of providential helps to the right understanding of the Bible" in the " irrefragable testimony of the Church."*

Tradition, not as supplementing, but as confirming Holy Scripture, is the uniform and consistent testimony of the undivided Church. It is not the authority of individual writers, who are often corrected by the general voice. It is not the teaching of isolated synods or particular portions of the Church. It is not a witness confined to one age alone, to the exclusion of other ages. If it is found to be unspeakably valuable and necessary, into what distinguished a place and office must we not set the Creeds, when we realize their character as the authorized embodiment of that universal testimony!

In the face of the Creeds the Church cannot introduce new doctrines, which were unknown from the beginning. They overthrow equally

---

* In Appendix to Sermon on *Primitive Tradition.*

the theory of objective development of doctrine and the theory of papal infallibility. Even if this latter did not swallow up the former, the true principle of tradition and a traditional Creed must nullify either. It stands in the way of any dogmatic decision in modern times by any portion of Christendom which makes revision of Creeds a possibility, which in fact already adds to their substantial teaching, which would cut away the present from the past and make our century a foreigner to the fourth. It is a rebuke to the doctrine which enthrones absolute irresponsibleness in the Church of God, and invests a single prelate of our day with a privilege of which the Apostles themselves knew nothing.

Catholic consent is our only hope of security in the matter of consistent Scriptural interpretation, and in that of doctrinal purity, and for that consent the Catholic Creeds stand. Across the waters of this dim and stormy world the articles of our belief are the trusted and unfading stars to light our way.

III.

The Creeds involve a complete and harmonious body of truth. To those who study them their various articles are seen to imply one another, to lead into one another, to complete and illustrate one another. If we trace their implications to their singular consequences, and then, as a corrective, to their mingled consequences; if we seek to discover their affinities and adjust their alliances; if we balance their inferences with all their constitutive elements; if we try to reach the interdependence of all their parts, we shall perceive how they shine with interior light. They are rightly open to speculation if we are already believers. As the Church first received the faith and then reasoned upon it, so must we. We must remember that they rest on the authority of God, and that they do not contradict, however much they may transcend, our reason. The duty of learning in order to believe is secondary only to that of believing in order to learn. St. Anselm said, "When we have arrived at faith, it is a piece of negligence to stop short of convincing ourselves, by the aid of thought, of that to which we have given credence." Within the circle of Catholic influence we do not need to dread speculation. The essence of rationalism consists, not in making reason a judge of evidence and a student of revealed truth, but in making it independent of authority. If a man judges concerning the Incarnation that it is impossible, he is a Rationalist; but if he tries to satisfy his reason so far as he may, why God became man, accepting the fact because it is revealed to the Church, he is no Rationalist. He believes that whatever is revealed must be true, like its Divine Revealer, and he may go on reverently to seek out its meaning, glad when he is permitted to wade somewhat further into the doings of the Most High, yet content when the guide Revelation will conduct the pupil Reason no further. The theologian speculates, but he remembers that the Church alone may dogmatize.

IV.

The Creeds are the inheritance of all portions alike of the Apostolic Church. It is therefore a matter for deep regret that the East and the West should declare the Nicene faith with even a single variation. The phrase "and the Son" added in the Article concerning the Holy Ghost and descriptive of His Eternal Procession, Spanish in its origin, accepted only in the West and never used by the East, has always been a grave scandal to the Oriental mind. It is no doubt a difference of language only, since all Christians acknowledge the Deity of the Holy Ghost, and it is not supposed by the Western Church to imply that He proceeds from the Son as from a Fountain in the same manner in which He proceeds from the Father. We cannot attain to reunion apart from the ancient Churches of the East, but so long as those Churches suppose the West to mean that the Holy Ghost proceeds from the Son as from the Original Source in the Godhead they will never come to terms. Either the West must be willing to give up the phrase as not being of universal reception, or the East must accept it on condition of the maintenance throughout the world of its true theological interpretation as meaning that the Holy Ghost proceeds from the Father through the Son. Except for that single discord there is a perfect harmony of faith, so far as the Nicene symbol can express it, in all parts of the Catholic world. One voice there is heard daily proclaiming from tens of thousands of altars the unchangeable convictions of Christ's visible body on earth. How is that voice affected by the existence in particular portions of the Church of doctrinal standards such as the Athanasian Hymn, which, though almost universal in the West, has never prevailed to any general extent in the East, and as the Trent decrees and the XXXIX Articles? We know how conscientious men feel bound in their several Communions by such expressions of the more restricted and subjective doctrinal life in those Communions, if not in the same degree as they feel bound by the ancient Creeds, yet still in a sense more or less defined to themselves.

When we enter a beautiful church we are at once struck by the general harmony of tone prevailing within it. There is a light there unlike the light we see anywhere else. It is not the light of the open sky, nor that of any houses we are accustomed to enter. It is a light peculiar to that particular building. It is caused by the harmonization of what streams through the windows with what dwells in the stone and wood and painted wall. When we stand before a single window and study its colors, its haloed forms, its mystic symbols, and the meaning that underlies it all, we see how different it is from the window we have just passed and from the window we just casually glance at beyond, in fact from any other window in the church. Yet its character and tone go to the making up of the peculiar quality of artistic and satisfying beauty we drink in with pensive eyes. But a study of effects will enable the artist to determine whether a lighter tint here would help the general harmony, or a darker there. The entire character of the interior may be modified by simple but subtle changes. In like manner we enter the great Apostolic Church of Jesus Christ. One great window there is, more dazzling and glorious than the others, like that east window in Gloucester Cathedral, in which the glass is "not only translucent, but is itself actually luminous with innumerable minute centres of radiation," because the "body of the glass is full of minute air bubbles, each of which holds the light and then reflects it out from the interior of the glass." That is the Creed window which gathers and sheds the Scripture glory that falls from the sun in the firmament above. The other windows are the decrees and catechisms and office-books of the various portions of the Church. That Creed window was framed and fashioned by the universal wisdom of the Christian mind; these others by isolated and estranged parts of it. There is a certain harmony withal, but all these side-lights must be brought entirely into tone with the great light and with one another. All interpretations of the past must be assimilated to the old expression of the Catholic mind. Each portion of the Church must submit to the united skill of all. Modifications must take place, but no true work of spiritual truth needs to be sacrificed. The work has to be done not by particular churches either for themselves or for others; but by all the elect, keeping in view the fact that each may learn from all in perfect submission to the guiding Spirit of truth and love.

It may be the notion of many who dream of reunion that it will bring with it the excision from the realm of doctrine of all liturgies, confessions, articles of doctrine, decrees of councils, writings of " Catholic fathers and ancient bishops "; but is it not much more reasonable to suppose that with the quickened intellect and fervent affection of a reunited Church, men's hold of the principles of truth would be so intensified that they would gather new light from every quarter, while purging from error their then common possession of a whole world of doctrinal literature? The Creeds must always remain what they are, but can never be restrained from bearing fruit in ever new and glorious forms of prayer and worship and saintly teaching.

The Church will not have a new faith, but she will always be apprehending more profoundly the old faith. She will be always applying her faith in the production of richer and riper thoughts to the exigencies of human life and the growing hopes of celestial pilgrims. Reunion cannot bring about a logical and practical divorce between what is fundamental and essential, and what is not. Experience proves that positive principles, on which alone reunion can be cemented, carry with them the seeds of very far-reaching effects. Even granting that in order to arrive at some possible basis of human device for reunion we could make the hypothetical distinction real and workable, it would vanish and be forgotten when the reunion had taken place. It is one thing to think we see clearly the distinction, and it is quite another to test the folly and peril of actually making the separation between the essential and that which grows out of it and is rooted in its very life and worthily shadows it forth. Some of the most unessential parts of a system perform a delicate office in making known the inward truth and reality of the essential. The Christian Year, for instance, would not be considered by anybody, I suppose, essential to the Church's existence, but what, among all the contrivances of men, could take its place as an instructor in the great principles of the Creeds?

If reunion ever comes within the limits of reasonable expectation, we cannot be blind to the lessons we have learned from our own past. We must conserve many things which have grown up with us and which once our Fathers far away got on without, but which, now that they have naturally sprouted from our Creeds, cannot be shorn away without doing an injury even to the Creeds themselves. Whence comes this prevalent fear of doctrinal statement? Definition is an evil only when carried on apart from the traditional life of the whole past, and under the spell of individualistic fancy. "Where matters have not been defined," says Bishop Forbes of Brechin, "men have generally contented themselves with the lower view; . . . we have seen how the faith of our own Church on the subjects that were left an open question has shrivelled and withered away."* Definition of like scope and dignity with that of the early Councils will hardly be again, but defi-

---

* *Explanation of the Nicene Creed*, Preface, p. vi.

nition on a great scale, comparable to the best doctrinal labors of the sixteenth century, will surely follow reunion, and the Church will choose as her authoritative language in the realms of anthropology and soteriology adequate expressions, already doubtless in being, to be raked out of the embers of forgotten learning, or discovered in the writings of our great divines.

The doctrinal standards peculiar to different portions of the Church of Christ have all had their share in producing the types of holy living to be found in those portions. Holy men of different communions do not indeed differ from one another in their characteristics so much as the doctrinal teachings of their communions differ, but still there is to be observed a tone, a fragrance, a beauty peculiar to some which cannot be found in others. The page which records the triumphs of Anglican sainthood is the fairest in Catholic annals. We do not need to apologize to any others. We have nothing to fear in contrast with any others. We have had our dark times, but what Church or body of Christians in the world have not had theirs? and I believe ours have been not a little overdrawn. Where shall we find, in days ancient or modern, in climes Northern or Southern, so glorious a type of piety as that moulded in the Anglican system—strong, yet tender, manly, yet full of sympathy, judicious, honest, wholesome, gracious, endued with sober and practical wisdom, full of a great dignity and a great simplicity, restrained, conservative, truthful in the depths of its spirit, contrasting to its own infinite advantage with almost any other types in Christian history. If it is insular, would that the whole world were an island!

The lamp of God never went out in our temple. What meek and lowly men have tended its pure flame! It would enchant your ears were I to read the precious diptychs. Where can the world equal that company which is represented by such names, to mention no others, as Hooker and Andrewes and Herbert and Hall and Hammond and Pearson and Sanderson, Taylor and Bramhall, Ken and Cosin and Granville and Gilpin and Sancroft and Wilson, Bull and Beveridge, Barrow and Butler, Jones and Cecil and Routh and Jolly and Pusey and Keble and Liddon?

Our Anglican mother has attributed to none of these maudlin miracles or exaggerated and impossible virtues, but she has formed them by her Prayer Book, her vernacular Scriptures, her parochial system, her learned priesthood, her unmutilated Eucharist, her incomparable Catechism, her family life—in a word, her system. Must we then give up a system, or see it greatly marred and broken, for the sake of obtaining what is, after all, not sure to come—the union of separated Christians? Is it not rather our duty to preserve our heritage for the sake not of our children only, but of our brethren also, who, like us, are of Anglo-Saxon blood and should have the blessings of the old Anglo-Saxon religion? We must learn ourselves from others what has seemed good and holy in their eyes and be ready to recognize anywhere the varied manifestations of God's grace, but when we read our own history and see what the system we have inherited has wrought, we must hesitate and think long before we begin to break up the timbers in our walls, if not some of the pavement beneath our feet. We all agree with Barrow that there are "points of less moment, more obscurely delivered, in which Christians may dissent, about which they may dispute, in which they may err, without breach of unity or prejudice to charity."* But let us ask, What has any portion of the Christian world to-day to give us in place of our minor beliefs and inferior rites that can compare with them in real practical efficiency toward producing the best type of holiness in our members? In the event of reunion we could not expect to have our system as a whole bound upon other portions of Christendom, nor to escape certain modifications ourselves by influences to which we could then oppose no barrier;

---

* Barrow on *Unity of the Church*. Works, vol. i., p. 763, Ed. of 1716.

but we need not be over-fearful that in such an event our experience of the very positive and superior advantages of our system would not be widely felt and recognized, and that it would not more than neutralize any counter influences. Rome and Constantinople must gain from Canterbury far more than they can ever give her; not that the whole Church will take on the Anglican complexion, but because the sturdy and vigorous character of the Anglican type must have a far-reaching permeation when once allowed equal limits of influence with other and less noble and more feeble types.

With reference to our Christian brethren, whose fathers went out from us in the past, we owe a great and imperative duty. We are bound to cherish our system, not out of a selfish pride in it, but because we truly believe it is fitted as no other system is to promote a calm and deeply religious character; but we must make the way for them to join with us as easy as we can. They have, we think, demonstrated their need of just what might be called our peculiar ways, and have themselves answered many of their former objections to our rites and ceremonies. The time seems ripe, not for giving up on every hand what has made us what we are, but for keeping our birthright. The tendency to the separatist idea and the separatist system has another tendency to Catholic ideas and usages more vital and enduring than itself to take account of. Our wisdom is to abide in our lot; to shun the unhealthy and belittling influences of party feeling; to look for, and haste, not unto earthly glories and religious ostracisms and degrees of arbitrary holiness graduated to degrees of ecclesiastical rank, but unto the coming of the day of God.

We must hold fast what we have, but we must also keep in men's minds that the Apostles' Creed is the Baptismal Creed, and that already all the baptized we call our own. We must lead them on, not by controversy, but by the example of humility and love. We cannot prefer unity to truth, nor compromise to the culture of a holy life. Intensive growth is the Church's first duty, afterward that which is extensive. But we can forget past differences, and look forward to happier and brighter days. This, which may seem to many a narrow and painfully inadequate, but I trust not a selfish or bigoted, view, will in due time prove to be the wisest and the best.

Even for the sake of unity we cannot listen on the one hand to proved imbecilities, nor on the other to certain degradation. We cannot abide those claims, which, even after the false decretals on which they were built up have been discredited in their native fields, are still gravely put forth with unbashful forehead before an astonished world; neither can we listen to possibilities which must leave us a sapless and inconsequent simulacre of Catholicity. Our plain duty is to forego mystic dreams of a golden age, and to keep on the noiseless tenor of our way. If superstitions, inanities, extravagances, have mingled with Christian teaching from the days of Hermas to those of Irving, and from the Araxes to the Rhine, we must be prepared still to behold many defects in the vision of a militant Church.

The Faith has survived the frantic and frigid philosophies with which Christians have played, and, untouched in its pure substance by optimism and pessimism, still holds forth the immaculate hope of life eternal through the love of God and the merits of our Blessed Redeemer; and we may be sure it will burn as a lamp until the end. There never was a time since St. Paul wrote to the Galatians when there were not sects and parties to trouble the peace of Christians, and I do not know why it should ever be otherwise so long as this mortal sphere of being rolls on its restless way. We are to labor for peace, and give ourselves unto prayer. We are to prove our religion by our lives, and then God, Who doeth all things well, will bring to pass His strange and wondrous act, whatever it may be. Sir Thomas Browne could never see a man pray, and not straightway fall to praying for him. So when we see men pray and lavish their gifts on missionary fields, and illustrate Christ's precepts in their daily walk, we may pray and give thanks likewise that God, Who is the Father of us all, will find a way to glorify His Son in us and in them together before the eyes both of angels and of men.

V.

When we turn the facts of our Christian faith into principles of our Christian life we see their deeper value and necessity. For what do they imply? Not Monism, with its condonation of human infirmity; not a code of Ethics grounded in the will and nature of no Eternal and Personal Being; not Positivism, that decayed folly, which told us that, while individual men perish at death, the race will go on for ever; not Materialism, that spent, insensate dream, which cared not even for the race, but whose one obstinate message was that physical death is the annihilation of thought; not Agnosticism, which now seems to have got so far as to admit a kind of intelligence in the Noumenon beyond phenomena, but cannot free itself from the old dictum by which it is fascinated, that there can be no communication from God to the world.

The Creeds have the majestic character of Him who said "I am the Truth," "I am from above." They carry with them the atmosphere of an eternal world. "God's word endureth for ever in heaven," and when we are shewn that surface and fringe of it which, in our finite limitation and present mortality we are capable of seeing, our nature revives and expands under the benignant influence. These mighty truths which the Church teaches abide in the realm of the unrevealed even while they are made to inhabit the realm of the revealed. They are mysteries, things, that is, which dwell at once in two spheres, a heavenly and an earthly. They are like the Person of Him Who came into the world to shew us the Father. They are Divine in their origin, and only earthly in their manifestation. What sublimity invests the mind which adoringly accepts them! They are not from beneath. They are not spun out of the brains of those who have divested themselves so far as they were able of all faith in the revealed religion. They are coals from the heavenly altar, whose intrinsic flame glows and waxes in our sight when the Spirit of illumination breathes on them as we pray. They are validities, not depending on time for their existence any more than the distinctions in the Godhead depend on Creation or Incarnation or the Church for theirs, but yet, like those distinctions, which exhibit themselves in Nature and Grace and the Means of Grace, clothe themselves in human speech, and make even the stones of the mountains and instruments of music to give them a kind of utterance. Such truths lift man's thoughts above that which is merely temporal. They tell him that he is a part of an enduring system, and that this is but "the bud of being." They set before him his whole life, and not a part of it, and that the least worthy part of it. In truth they set forth God as the life of men, and reveal His Being as eternal and His Nature as love. They shew the condescension of God in the Person of the Son, Who came to unite heaven and earth and God and man, and to make our mortal years a fair image of His unspotted eternity. They bring the message of a real forgiveness and a real hope to all who will repent and believe. They open the gate of heaven's kingdom even here and now. They do not tell man merely of a life to come, but mingle that life with his earthly life. They do not tell him of promises merely, but of present privileges. They tell him not only of the first Adam created in sinless liberty, but also of the Second Adam bringing perfect attainment into view. They shew him the symmetry and ripeness of his being—man brought from capacity to capability, from liberty to freedom, from hope to fulfilment, from possibility to attainment—they exhibit holiness as the matured fruit of a long process of sanctification, as arrival at that ultimate stage of spiritual life where there are no salient virtues and graces, because all virtues and graces complete one another; as the diffusion of spiritual tone through the entire life, as will and affections and intellect all wrought to one stedfast strength and lustre, till it is impossible to connect more or less of blessedness with one than with another part of his nature; as Nature's discovered equilibrium and point of rest, as unity of life in itself and in its Divine original, as satisfaction with Christ's glorified likeness, as fulness of joy and pleasure for evermore.

These mysteries of our faith teach that holiness is the direct effect in man's nature of the Holy Spirit's working, Who dwells in Christ's members, that it is a condition which implies, supplements and hallows earthly schemes of morality, that it is a supernatural cause affecting the entire nature of a man, that it is man dedicated to God and then consecrated by God, and using his natural faculties in a supernatural strength, that it is man living under the monition of the Holy Ghost, and through the continuous impartation of vitality from that gracious Guest, that it is, in fine, the effect of the constant ministration of Christ to man by the Spirit which dwelt in and glorified the humanity of Christ.

Is not such a revealed faith fitted to lift man up for ever, especially when it is received and made his own by means of the ministries of grace? As

Keble said at Winchester in 1830, "We cannot separate the means of grace from the doctrines of grace." Is not this the Faith by believing which men wrought righteousness, obtained promises, quenched the violence of fire, escaped the edge of the sword, out of weakness were made strong? Is not this the Faith needed in the world to-day, when there is certainly a recrudescence of Pagan ideals and sentiments, when there are multitudes in Christian lands who hear no longer the doctrines of the Catholic faith, but are entertained by incoherent magnificences and undigested hypotheses, and with heresies taken bodily out of Valentinian workshops, or imbibed in "the tents of Pelagius"?

Christ incarnate, crucified, glorified; Christ in us the hope of glory; Christ, revealing the Father and ministered by His Holy Spirit; Christ, uniting the whole family in heaven and earth in Himself, is the only hope of man. Him the Church adores, Him the Creeds confess, Him the Scriptures delineate, Him the Sacraments convey, Him the Apostolic priesthood represents, Him the world desires, Him the sinful need, Him the saints follow, Him the Father loves.

The Creeds that guard and set forth the ineffable truth concerning Him are of priceless value, both in themselves and in their history. The Catholic Church can never part with these. It is inconceivable that the least word in them will ever be exscinded. They are sacred symbols, because they are the Church's deliberate witness to the truth of Christ's Person and grace.

VI.

The Church of which we are members is a part of the visible Catholic Church throughout all the world. It believes that the Church is a Divine structure, built on Jesus Christ our only Saviour, and animated by His Spirit of truth and holiness. It does not imagine that the Church's truest and deepest unity has ever been broken, but only that its perfect outward form has been impaired in the course of the Christian centuries. It does not attempt to affirm that external unity is any longer a fact. It believes that such unity should, by God's help, be restored. But it cannot exhibit or invent any hypothetical or tentative basis for Christians to stand on together. It can only point to the foundations laid long ago. The Anglican Communion cannot depart from the principles of the Catholic Church, of which she is a sound and living part. She is subject to the Church in its undivided capacity, so that whatever it has at any time professed, she must profess; and whatever it has at any time rejected, she must reject. She cannot have anything to do with laying a foundation for reunion, or for Christian unity, if by that is meant a federation of Christian organizations. For the foundation standeth sure. Unless the believers everywhere will look on Catholic principles not as separable bases, any number of which may be taken to build upon, but as essential one to another, and as all standing or falling together, and as carrying with them the interpretation which their whole history affords of them, we must be content to wait. Our Church has the future in her hands if only she can be patient and be true to herself. She must sacrifice present palpability to future reality. She must be pardoned for looking at this matter from within and not from without. She is eighteen hundred years of age, and her memory teems with her history in all its parts and periods. Side-lights from forgotten ages teach her a theory of conservatism scarcely to be appreciated by those whose roots do not run through all the past. We may be sure that when the Protestant bodies are ready to receive the Historic Episcopate, they will be ready also to accept in the main what in the course of time has grown up with and out of that Episcopate. We cannot afford to risk internal schism for the sake of obtaining what at best might be a temporary union of some Christian societies. We cannot give up certainties for uncertainties.

"The dog that snapt the shadow dropt the bone." The four propositions of the Anglican

Bishops, if read in their bare outline, are untenable and must remain unfruitful. If looked at with an eye to their history, they will be found to carry a necessarily Catholic and historic interpretation. The Bishops meant, no doubt, to hint at concessions and accommodations; they never could have meant that there is no universal and well-known doctrine of a visible Kingdom of our Redeemer among men, having authority in matters of faith; and that there is no universal and well-known doctrine of sacramental grace and Apostolic orders and Scriptural interpretation. Men in general must have a more profound knowledge of the Christian past, until they can breathe its atmosphere and see with its eyes, before they can safely approach this question of unity. Walter Savage Landor told us that we must see through former ages before we can see through our own. We do not want the accidental past, but the essential. We do not wish to restore Mediævalism, nor Byzantinism; but we want to live our modern American life with the wisdom which eighteen centuries of Christian thought and culture have accumulated. Our work is in the present, but our experience is in the past. We do not wish to forget either our duty or our education. The present age differs from past ages only in the accidental shows of things. The heart of the world is the same it always was. The need of the world is the same it always was. We may profit by the failures as well as by the successes of our fathers. Let us not be led away in so great a matter by emotion. Let us not anticipate the order of Divine Providence. Let us not build a tower until we know whether we can finish it. Let us not mistake our hopes for realities. You will remember that when Israel, Judah and Edom together opposed the Moabites, they filled some trenches with water, which, reddened by the morning sun, seemed in the eyes of the latter from the heights above like pools of blood. Supposing their foes to have quarrelled with and slain one another, they sallied down to plunder the camp and were defeated. We want hope and zeal, but we want also a sober judgment. We want unity but we want to be sure no rotten beams or crumbling stones get into the foundation. We want, before all, humility and patience; humility, that we may not trust ourselves too far where vast issues are at stake, and patience, that we may bear with the ignorant and self-willed. In a word, we want by God's unspeakable mercy the gift of a sound and loving mind to seek and set forward His Kingdom among men in the fulness of its privileges, in the greatness of its design, in the untold might of all its healing and renewing power.

The Two Great Sacraments.

LECTURE IV.

VEN. A. ST. JOHN CHAMBRÉ, D.D.,

ARCHDEACON OF LOWELL, AND DEAN OF CONVOCATION.

THE TWO GREAT SACRAMENTS.

OUR Lord Jesus Christ founded the Christian Church. It was potential in Him in all its fulness, and in all its divine prerogatives, powers and influences, for all the world and for all the ages. He called, taught, trained, disciplined, a college of Apostles, to promulgate what He delivered unto them, to do what He commanded should be done, to evangelize the nations, to build up the Church, *His* Church. The Church was complete in the essentials of its organization, while our Lord lived on earth. He completed His teaching, and perfected the organization, it may be affirmed, during those memorable days between the Resurrection and the Ascension. On the Day of Pentecost, in accordance with His promise and prophecy, the Holy Ghost descended upon the Church, to abide with it for ever, and to lead it into all truth. Beginning at Jerusalem, then, thousands were converted, and there were added to the Church daily those who were in the process of being saved, and these all "continued steadfastly in the Apostles' doctrine and fellowship, and in the breaking of the bread, and in the prayers." Thence the Gospel of the kingdom spread, throughout Judea, in Samaria, across the mountains into Asia Minor, beyond the Euphrates eastward, across the Ægean Sea into Greece, thence into Italy, even into great Rome itself, and westward into Spain and beyond. Within thirty years, substantially, all this was accomplished, and before a line of the New Testament was written. It was the New Jerusalem let down from God out of Heaven. It soon changed the face of the world. In the world, it was not of the world—it was everywhere a divine kingdom within every earthly kingdom.

Thus, the Christian Church is a divine, not a human, institution. It is not a voluntary association or guild, such as men may make or unmake, with which they may or may not connect themselves with no vital consequences in either case, or which they may erect or strike down at pleasure. It is the Church of the living God, built upon foundations of prophets and apostles, Jesus Christ Himself being the chief Corner-Stone, and the promise and assurance is, that the gates of hell shall not prevail against it. This divinely constituted Church, this kingdom of God in the world, is called, historically, Holy, Apostolic and Catholic.

Holy—as set apart, separate from the world, from the world-spirit, and all that dominates the world, and sanctified to God, and to all pure and blessed usages and purposes. It trains immortal souls spiritually. It conserves the knowledge, and worship, and service of God.

Apostolic—because built upon the Apostles as upon foundation-stones. The Apostles carried everywhere the Gospel, and planted everywhere the Church, organized into congregations of the faithful. They transmitted the orders, teachings, mission and jurisdiction committed to them, in a line that has not been broken for a moment from the beginning. Apostolic government, discipline, doctrine, fellowship, sacramental rites and methods, make the Church apostolic, to all of which witness the New Testament, the œcumenical councils, the great bishops and doctors, east and west, and all sacred history from the days when the Church began.

Catholic. The blessed Lord gave a religion for the world. It is a religion greater and better than the world possessed before, or has possessed since apart from it. Judaism was racial, national, necessarily and inevitably. The chosen people were called out of the world to be in covenant relations with God, thus witnesses to Him as the one true God, and a preparation for the day of the Lord. Judaism gave way, as it was not and could not be Catholic. No Pagan system ever was or could be Catholic—it could be but tribal, or, at the most, national. But the kingdom of God, the Church, is to compass all nations and kindreds and tribes and peoples, that every knee may bow to God, and every tongue confess to Him. Jesus Christ is the Light to lighten the Gentiles, as well as the glory of His people Israel. His commission is:— "Go ye into all the world, and preach the Gospel to every creature." "The Church," St. Cyril tells us, "is called Catholic, because it extends through all the world, from one end of the earth to the other." But this is not all that is involved in the word Catholic. The word *Church* defines the word *Catholic* as really as the word Catholic describes the Church. The Church is a divine and visible organization, not an idea, or condition, intangible, invisible, inorganic. It has its divinely called and consecrated Ministry, instituted by Jesus Christ. This Ministry is self-perpetuating, three-fold in character, bishops (as successors of the Apostles), priests and deacons. It has a specific doctrine or system of doctrines, called the Gospel, which, as communicated explicitly or implicitly by the blessed Lord, is His, and like Himself is the same yesterday, to-day and for ever. It cannot be changed, but in its essential features and statements of facts remains unalterable from generation to generation, unto the end of time. This Gospel may be called old. It *is* old—old as the purpose of God to save a fallen, sinful race—old as the time when His eternal and only Son took upon Him our nature, and was born of a pure Virgin, that He might unite humanity with Himself, and offer propitiation and atonement for the sins of the whole race. But the Gospel remains for ever new, for it applies to each generation as it comes and goes, for its spiritual life and salvation. Nothing can be added to it or taken from it. There can be nothing read into it that does not, by the consentient voice of the Church, belong to it, and nothing can be read out of it that from the beginning was put there by the Holy Ghost. There is no new Gospel, and there cannot be. What is true in Christianity is true from the beginning, and is not new. What is new, in the sense of being otherwise than Christianity has ever been, is not true. The Catholic Church holds the Faith and Order and Polity which were in the beginning, the same everywhere, and always, and continually. Where this Faith, Order and Polity obtain, there is the Catholic Church. "Catholic" means not only universality, and thus comprehensiveness, but apostolic doctrine and fellowship and discipline. It is, therefore, exclusive as well as inclusive. It excludes those who reject the faith—rather they exclude themselves. The Holy, Apostolic, Catholic Church does not include heresy, and cannot comprehend it within its system.

Again, Catholicity stands for unity. The Church is One, naturally and inevitably. For a thousand years this oneness prevailed. Then, owing to geographical and political conditions mainly, and in a measure to differences which gradually developed, this oneness, outwardly, ceased to exist, and the Church was known as Eastern or Western, Greek or Latin. Then the Western or Latin Church was riven, and, outwardly, communion ceased between the Roman and Anglican expressions of the Church. But whatever the conditions, and however apart these Communions may appear to be, they each and all preserve those essential features stamped upon the Church in the beginning by Our Blessed Lord and His Apostles. With whatever variations, they continue in the Apostolic Doctrine and Fellowship, and in the breaking of the Bread, and in the prayers. They constitute the outward, visible, organic, historic Church of the Living God—and practically dominate the Christian world. Our own Anglican Branch, having its roots in England since the second century after Christ, long before there was an organized and consolidated English nation, may well be taken—is taken by ourselves—

as the purest and nearest akin to the primitive times. To its standard, the other great Branches will, in God's time and way, undoubtedly draw nigh. There will be no Christian unity otherwise. It occupies a vantage ground to this end, which Greek and Latin are more and more, however sometimes ungraciously and however slowly, confessing in explicit or in implicit terms.

Thus far, we have the Church set before us as a divinely instituted, visible, organic Body, with a divinely instituted Ministry, and a divinely enunciated doctrine or teaching. Through this organism, this Church, God is acting upon the world to save the world and to bring it to Himself, redeemed in Jesus Christ. For definite purposes which will unfold themselves, the Church has possessed, from the first, certain characteristic, outward, visible, in essential features unvarying, actions. They are vital, integral factors in the very being of the Church, conserving its life and teaching, and enabling it to be effective in the spiritual uplifting of human souls. We call these "Sacraments." I am to speak of "The Two Great Sacraments." These Sacraments have been ordained by Jesus Christ, the Great Head of the Church, and by Him it is commanded that they shall be continually administered by the Church to the end of the ages. As these were not originated by men, but by Our Blessed Lord,

they are not subject to the will of men. They are
also unchangeable, in any way that may affect
their essential nature or purpose, by any man, or
any body of men, or even by the Church itself.
They are to be retained, observed, administered,
as the Lord directed, in the form and with the
matter (elements) ordained by Him. They enter
thus into the very constitution of the Church.
The Bishops of the Anglican Communion specifically recognize this. These Sacraments are part
of the Deposit entrusted to the Episcopate, "to
be ministered with unfailing use of Christ's words
of institution, and of the elements ordained by
Him." They are thus made an essential article
to be accepted as a basis upon which there can be
any hope of ever effecting Christian unity, or of
conserving the integrity of the One, Holy, Catholic, Apostolic Church.

WHAT IS A SACRAMENT?

The Latin *Sacramentum* refers to a military
oath of obedience and allegiance. The taking of
this oath was often attended with much of religious ceremony, to make it the more impressive
and awe-inspiring. To violate that oath would
be treason, the greatest crime of which a soldier
could be guilty. As binding obligations are taken
by Christians to their Lord, both in Holy Baptism
and the Holy Eucharist, there is seen at once the

force and the propriety of this word as used by the Church. The word *Sacramentum*, moreover, is the equivalent of the Greek μυστήριον or "mystery." This word the Church used from the beginning. The language of the Church, at the first, crystallized in the Greek. The New Testament was written in Greek; the early Liturgies were Greek; it was the language of the intercourse of the Eastern world. As Christianity passed to the West, and took root among Latin-speaking peoples, a change took place. The Bible was rendered into Latin. The great Western Fathers began to write in that tongue—it became the Church language of the West, and so continues in the Roman obedience unto this day. The Greek still continues the Church language of the East. The Anglican Church, as a part of the Western Church, has rendered its services into English, but borrows naturally many of its terms from the Latin. By the Greek, μυστήριον was applied to any service to which only the initiated, or those properly prepared, were admitted. The idea of a great, spiritual meaning, not known to nor discernible by everybody, was at the root of this usage. Holy Baptism was a mystery, for the reception and understanding of which, on the part of adults, preparation was essential—and only the baptized could be, or ever were, admitted to the Holy Eucharist. Precisely this was the idea in the West, and in this way the West used the word *Sacramentum*.

The Greek Church recognizes seven sacraments: so does the Western Church. These are Holy Baptism, Confirmation, the Holy Eucharist, Holy Orders, Matrimony, Penance, and Extreme Unction. Neither in the Greek Church, however, nor in the Roman, is the same emphasis laid upon each of these: there are the greater and the lesser. There are two that rise above all the rest—Holy Baptism and the Supper of the Lord. We are concerned in this lecture with these only. Now the general Christian definition of a Sacrament in its highest phase is, that it is "an outward and visible sign of an inward and spiritual grace," or, as it is called by St. Augustine, "the sign of a sacred thing." These two Sacraments are declared as "generally necessary to salvation"—in the explanation of which it may be sufficient to say, that they are necessary to salvation, if they can be obtained. These two were assuredly and specifically instituted by the Blessed Saviour Himself, and were commanded by Him to be used in His Church for ever. "He that is baptized," He declares, "shall be saved." His command to His Apostles was "Go ye into all the world . . . baptizing . . . in the Name of the Father, and of the Son, and of the Holy Ghost." "This do," or "offer," He directed the Apostles, when He instituted the

Holy Eucharist, by taking bread and breaking it —"this do, in remembrance of me." "Drink all ye of this," He said, when He took the cup and blessed it. "This is my Body," He said of the bread. "This is my Blood," He said of the wine. His words also are, "Except ye eat of my flesh and drink of my blood, ye have no life in you"— the life of God is not in us.

In the sixteenth century, when the Church of England asserted its independence of Rome, it restored the cup to the laity. It then gradually eliminated accretions which had gathered from the conditions and circumstances through which the Church had passed, in what are called the "Dark Ages." Some of these accretions had in a measure obscured the full significance of these two great Sacraments, which the Church of England now emphasized in the strongest language. It did not, however, deny the sacramental character of the other "five commonly called Sacraments," but of these two the Church is explicit in its teachings. They are "ordained of Christ." They are not "badges or tokens" merely of our "Christian profession." They are "certain sure witnesses and effectual signs of grace and God's good will towards us," and by them He "quickens" and also "strengthens and confirms our faith in Him." The Catechism expressly declares the meaning of a sacrament to be an "outward and visible sign of an inward and spiritual grace given unto us: ordained by Christ Himself, as a means whereby we receive the same, and a pledge to assure us thereof." This definition is most carefully worded. There is an outward and visible sign to a Sacrament—the sign of an inward and spiritual grace *given unto us;* that grace answers to that sign: the sign must suggest it, the grace must be conformed to it. The outward and visible sign and the inward and spiritual grace are constituent elements of the Sacrament, mutually dependent and interdependent.

1. Lustration by water was not used for the first time by our Lord. What He did was to adopt the Rite and adapt it to His purpose, and ordain and constitute it a Christian Sacrament. The Baptism of John was with water, but it was not Christian Baptism. His was merely a symbolic Rite, signifying adherence to a new teaching and a life in accordance therewith. In the Baptist's view it was also, no doubt, a preparation for the incoming Kingdom of God, and so for the remission of sins. The Blessed Lord was baptized of John to emphasize John's relation to Him as His forerunner. He needed not that Baptism otherwise. He was without sin, and required no cleansing therefrom. The fact remains, therefore, that Baptism is a Sacrament of the Church, ordained as such by Jesus Christ. From His time to ours it has been

in the Church, the door of entrance to the Church, for men, women and children. Unfailingly, water has been used, and the baptismal Formula. Valid Baptism is found in the use of water, whether by immersion, pouring or sprinkling, "in the Name of the Father, and of the Son, and of the Holy Ghost." To what end? Thereby is the Church enlarged and perpetuated. It brings into new relations and new conditions in a new kingdom. Jesus Christ has established a kingdom, His Church. Everyone brought into it must be consecrated, set apart for it and in it. Being born naturally into the world, we are born by Baptism supernaturally into the kingdom of God's Son, and have the washing of regeneration. This is the "New Birth," which, of course, is not to be confounded with the doctrine of conversion or the doctrine of sanctification, *i.e.*, growth in grace. Holy Baptism brings out of the birth-estate of sin in the world into a state of grace in Christ's kingdom, and we are thereby made "members of Christ, children of God, and inheritors of the kingdom of Heaven." We are thus "grafted" into the body of Christ, who is the "Head of the body, the Church"—grafted into Christ Himself. These new relations and conditions are correctly expressed by the word "regenerate"—re-generate—re-made—no longer a child of the world, but a child of the Church and of God. Jesus Christ is the Eternal

Son of God, God's only Son. By Baptism we are made one with Christ, are adopted into the family of God, and become heirs of God, and joint heirs with Christ of all that God can give or do in Him. We become one compact body with Him and with each other and with God. "Except a man be born of water and of the Spirit, he cannot enter into the kingdom of God"; is not a member of the Holy, Catholic and Apostolic Church. Observe still, and carefully, that Holy Baptism as a Sacrament, administered as Christ ordained, is the "outward and visible sign of an inward and spiritual grace *given unto us.*" It is given to us in and through that Baptism. The inward and spiritual grace is a divine power of the Holy Ghost, whereby we die unto sin and live unto Christ. The old man is put off and the new man is put on. Birth sin is washed away, and the soul starts anew, with the power of an endless life infused, a spiritual grace implanted, which, if used, brings the soul under subjection to God, and enables it to grow up into Christ in all things. We may not know how this change is effected or how this power operates, but the fact remains. "The wind bloweth where it listeth and we hear the sound thereof, but cannot tell whence it cometh or whither it goeth. So is every one that is born of the Spirit." We have the assurance of Jesus Christ Himself as to all this. We are baptized into Him; His life takes possession of our life, unless we reject Him or are unfaithful to Him. The Church is a body of baptized persons, baptized after the manner, and with the matter ordained by the Lord. These constitute the Church, the Body of the Faithful—the Church that is Holy, Apostolic, Catholic, the Church on earth and in Heaven, the Church of all the ages. This Sacrament of Holy Baptism, therefore, cannot be yielded, cannot be abrogated. It is a deposit which the Church holds, which the Church must administer, and which by and through the Church only can be validly bestowed. It is a very different thing, as may be at once discerned, from that which is sometimes called Baptism, but which is either otherwise administered than as Christ ordained, or is robbed of all the meaning and efficacy which are attached to it by the teaching of Revelation or by the consciousness of the Church. In the mind of the Church it is not the sign declarative of a pre-existing fact, nor even a symbolic setting forth of what is ideally desirable. It takes man out from the world and from the state of sin in which he is born into the world, and makes him a citizen of the kingdom of God, with the old life blotted out, and a new life begun. It is God's provision, in His infinite mercy, by which there is now union with Him in Christ, and with the saints of all ages, past and present and to come. It is the sprinkling of the blood of the New Covenant, by which the soul is made white in the light of the glorified Lord.

2. The great Sacrament of Holy Baptism, however, but introduces into the kingdom of God, in a regenerate state and under new conditions and in new relations, and is thus but a preparation for the life of that kingdom, which is a continuous kingdom. In that kingdom there must needs be the perpetual reaching out and on, until there shall be attained the stature of perfection in Christ Jesus the Lord. To this end there must be the perpetual nourishing and strengthening of the new and Divine life, that it fail not, but that it may increase more and more unto the perfect day, from glory unto glory. For this, provision is made in that other great Sacrament, also ordained by Christ. This Sacrament stands for much besides this—stands for the conservation and the presentation of the Incarnation, and the Sacrifice, and the Atonement, and for the wonder and power and glory of them—but it stands also for this. It has various designations.

It is called (*a*) "The Eucharist," as signifying the giving or returning thanks, thus a Thanksgiving, or Thank-Offering. This term is used alike in the Eastern and Western Church.

It is called (*b*) "A memorial," because the essential meaning of the words "This do in remembrance of me" is, "This offer as a Memorial of me,"—of course, a Memorial before God. The word "do" is properly "offer," and as such is used repeatedly in the Greek version of the Old Testament. To "offer" is a term of sacrifice, the "Sacrifice of the Altar." A sacrifice is anything, living or otherwise, submitted to God in whatever way, as a religious offering. For whatever else this Sacrament exists, it exists to "show the Lord's death"; but His death was a sacrificial offering to God "for us men and for our salvation." He was the "Lamb slain from the foundation of the world," and now, in His glory, is represented as a "Lamb as if slain" in the presence of God for us, and pleading His sacrifice of Himself. This idea of sacrifice inheres in the very constitution of this Sacrament. "This is my Body," broken for you. "This is my Blood," shed for you. His Body was offered on the Cross, and there His Blood flowed for humanity. It is therefore rightly called a Sacrifice, a Memorial Sacrifice because it brings before us *His* Sacrifice; it represents (re-presents) that Sacrifice, not only before us but before God, as Christ Himself, our Great High Priest, for ever pleads before the Throne the offering of Himself upon the Altar of Calvary. This is not, however, and must not be assumed as, a *repetition* of the Sacrifice of the Cross, or any the least renewal of Christ's sufferings or of His death. His sacrificial death was once for all, not only for all men, but for all time, and can never be repeated. He made, once for all, a "full, perfect, and sufficient sacrifice, oblation and satisfaction for the sins of the whole world."

It is called (*c*) "a Communion." The Faithful partake of it, as did the Apostles when it was first instituted. Together we partake—partake of one Bread, or Loaf, broken, and of one Cup—thus declaring that we are one with Christ, one redeemed family in Him, feeding on the Bread of Heaven and the Wine of God, which is *One* Christ. It is a feast upon a sacrifice—and thus, a Communion. The Paschal Supper was eaten and ended; and the type, finding its fulfilment in Christ, ceased, and the new Rite was ordained to take its place, and to show forth the One Lamb of God who was slain for us.

By whatever name called, however, each designation bringing out some special feature and emphasizing it, the essential nature and meaning of this Sacrament remain. As a Sacrament, there is the outward and visible sign, and the inward and spiritual grace. It is a "mystery"; but a mystery is always something that is known in part, but of which something remains unknown until revealed. As the outward and visible sign we have the Bread and Wine. The inward and spiritual grace, given to us in and through the sign, consists in the Body and Blood of Christ, "spiritually taken and received by the Faithful," so that there is the "strengthening and refreshing of our souls by the Body and Blood of Christ, as our bodies are by the bread and wine." There is here no definition of how the Lord is present in the Sacrament, or how He is received by us, or how we are strengthened and refreshed, but the fact is clearly stated. We receive the Body and Blood sacramentally, and are sacramentally built up in Christ. The Sacrament is not, therefore, and cannot be, merely a memorial—something which simply reminds of Christ. In that view, there is no sacramental character or efficacy, no spiritual vitality, or grace, or virtue. On the other hand, as already stated, there is no renewal here of Christ's personal sacrifice. To sustain that view, Transubstantiation would be in complete harmony, and must needs be accepted. But Transubstantiation, in any real sense, there is not in this Sacrament. That would involve not only the constant and multitudinous repetition of the death of Our Blessed Lord, but a constantly recurring miracle for which there is no precedent, no occasion, and no authority. On the theory of Transubstantiation, so awful, so appalling are the possible dangers involved in the administration of the Cup, that the withdrawal of the Cup from the laity is justified,—even in view of the fearful consequences involved in what may then be a mutilated Sacrament.

"The Bread which we break is a partaking of the Body of Christ; and likewise the cup of blessing is a partaking of the Blood of Christ." But "the Body of Christ is given, taken, and eaten, in the Supper, only after an heavenly and spiritual manner." There is a "Real Presence" of Our Blessed Lord in this Sacrament, not a *real absence*. We partake of *Him*. We commemorate His sacrificial death for us. We plead before the Throne of God His propitiatory offering, for ourselves, for the whole Church, and for the whole world. It is the One Bread broken, and the One Cup of the New Covenant in His Blood, witnessing our unity each with the other, with our Saviour, and with our God.

Clearly, any essential change in this Sacrament as to the "sign" (the elements used, the method of using them, and the words of consecration) would endanger the character of the Sacrament, and thus invalidate its efficacy. It would cease to be what was instituted by Christ, and could no longer be held as a witness or a channel of any inward and spiritual grace given unto us. This is true, also, of course, of the other great Sacrament, Holy Baptism. These Sacraments, as divinely instituted, as ordained by Christ Himself, have supernatural virtues, whether we will have it so or not. The Christian religion is a supernatural religion. It has no meaning otherwise that we are under obligation to recognize. It must be supernatural, as dealing with God and His relations with men, with the soul and its relations to God, with spiritual verities, and spiritual life, and an immortal destiny. The alternative is logical and necessary—either the Christian religion is a supernatural religion, or there is no such thing as a Christian religion. Whatever pertains essentially, therefore, to this religion, may well be, and must be, taken as channels or instruments of conveying supernatural efficacies. The consciousness of the Greek Church was not astray when it called, as it still calls, the sacraments by the word "Mystery." Nor was the consciousness of the Latin Church astray when it called, as it still calls, these mysteries "Sacraments," and defined a Sacrament as the "sign of a sacred thing," or the "external sign of an inward grace." Moreover, as by the great mysteries of Holy Baptism and the Lord's Supper, our souls are bound to Christ, to live to Him and for Him in loving obedience to His holy will, as the great Captain of our salvation, the ancient meaning of the word *Sacramentum* stands out boldly. The Sacraments are to us, in very truth, the oaths of our allegiance to God in Christ Jesus our Lord, as soldiers of the Cross, to fight the good fight until the world shall be subject to Him by the witness we give, or until we shall die in the battle for victory over all that opposes itself against Him as rightfully the Lord of lords, and the King of kings.

As with the Sacrament of Holy Baptism, so with the Sacrament of the Holy Eucharist. It is a deposit received by the Church, to be conserved by the Church, and transmitted unimpaired by the Church through the ages. It is for the sustenance of human souls brought into union with Jesus Christ by Baptism. It is the impartation of Christ Himself to the souls of the faithful; by virtue of which we become bone of His bone, flesh of His flesh, blood of His blood, until those who are in Him, individually and collectively, shall be changed into His glorious image, as one body, transfigured and resplendent. The Catholic, Apostolic Church cannot yield this Sacrament, or vary or alter it in any essential feature, or make it, in any way or sense, other than it is, and as it has received it. To do so would involve the spiritual impoverishment and gradual decline and death of the Church itself. As the Church is able to give, in the Sacrament of Baptism, union with Christ, and so with God, and with all saints living here or beyond the stars, so it gives, in the Sacrament of the Body and Blood of Christ, the very life of Christ Himself, which thus flows through all lives of all saints, everywhere and forever, holding their lives as one life, an eternal life, ever enlarging as it rolls on, and ever gathering to itself the fulness of the blessedness and purity, the joy and peace of Heaven. Upon these two great Sacraments the Episcopate rightly insists. These the Church only can bestow in all their fulness; these it is willing and anxious, as trustee for God, to bestow upon all those who will accept. These Sacraments are now, as they have ever been, the bonds of the Catholic Church, holding it fast to the faith of Christ. When they shall be rightly understood, appreciated and accepted, when all who profess and call themselves Christians, but who are now away from or outside of the historic Church of the Living God, shall become obedient to them, they will be found the uniting powers that will bring again the scattered remnants of the spiritual Israel, the broken fragments of Christendom, and there will be once more one Fold and one Shepherd, one Faith and one Church.

Obviously, this view of these two Sacraments, being essentially the view held by the historic Church, East and West, by the Greek Church and its dependencies, the Latin Church and its constituencies, and the Anglican Church wherever scattered abroad, must be preserved intact by us. Certainly this must be, if we would aid in furthering the cause of a universal and abiding Christian unity, so devoutly to be desired, or if there shall be any hope of securing that unity. To yield these Sacraments, by the toning down of their meaning or power, or by admitting in association with them views quite commonly held, would be the emphasizing of lines divergent from the great Catholic bodies of the world, and would make the consummation of *their* reunion impossible. We should lose then the vantage-ground which it is believed that we now possess in furthering the accomplishment of the unity of Catholic Christendom. A unity of Protestant Christendom would be but partial unity after all. The bishops of this Church of ours never meant, and could not mean, to sever themselves from the Catholic heritage which is theirs, and so make more formidable and more hopeless the divergencies which now exist. The fulness of the sacramental idea, as held in the Church from the beginning, is ours, and the blessings inherent therein. These Sacraments we offer in all loving sincerity and earnestness to our non-Episcopal brethren of whatever name, assured that the acceptance of the Sacramental idea will serve to unify them, and the sooner and more surely lead to a possible unity in the faith and Person of our Lord Jesus Christ in the one Holy Catholic and Apostolic Church. One Lord, one Faith, one Baptism, one nourishment of the soul by the Body and Blood of Christ, one God and Father of us all—this is the goal to which we may and ought to press. This is the divine ideal of the Church on earth. This will be the realization of the Church in Heaven. We have a Baptism which makes members of Christ and of His Church. We have an altar, and the priests of God everywhere offer the Sacrifice as the great and central act of the worship of the Church—which it has been from the beginning. It is everywhere, as it has ever been—the pleading of *His* atoning sacrifice upon the cross, Who prayed that all who named His Name might be one with each other, and one with Him, and one with God.

The Historic Episcopate.

LECTURE V.

THE REV. FRANCIS J. HALL, M.A.,

Instructor of Theology in the Western Theological Seminary, Chicago, Ill.

THE HISTORIC EPISCOPATE.

It is my privilege to address you concerning the Historic Episcopate.

I need not labor to convince you of the importance of the subject. The air is full of it. Christians of every name are wrestling with the problem of Church Unity; and the sectarian world about us considers our insistence upon the Historic Episcopate to be the chief barrier to unity, while our own Bishops have asserted that Ministry to be "incapable of compromise or surrender." It is clear that no unity is possible between parties thus opposed to each other, until the claims of the Historic Episcopate have been duly examined and an agreement has been reached as to their validity.

Other issues are involved in this controversy, and of vital nature. It is a fact that the rejection of the Episcopate has been followed sooner or later by heresy, decay of faith in the doctrine of supernatural grace, disintegration and unbelief. To one who believes in the doctrine of Apostolic Succession this seems perfectly natural; for what is more logical and inevitable than that such results should follow upon a loss of the Ministry— and the only Ministry—which God has ordained and empowered to guard the Faith, dispense the means of grace, and hold the faithful together in unity until the end of days?*

The subject of the Historic Episcopate necessarily has peculiar interest for us. The Protestant world invites us to justify the attitude assumed by our Bishops in their Declaration of Unity, wherein they insist upon the Episcopate as upon an *ultimatum*, refusing to compromise or surrender it even when called upon to do so for the sake of unity and charity. This invitation is a natural one; and, if we would avoid appearance of evil, we must give a sufficient reason for our position, and one equivalent to religious necessity. Nothing short of this will justify the setting forth of an *ultimatum* as to the course to be pursued in restoring visible unity to the Church of God.

In order to exhibit such a reason we may be obliged to display truths and convictions which

---

* Haddan's *Apostolical Succession in the Church of England*, 1883, pp. vi., 19-22.

are not acceptable to those who question us. But in such case, the interests of honor as well as of charity will require that we should lay bare the true nature of the hindrances in this direction which must be removed before unity can be secured.

It is my purpose to exhibit as well as I can (*a*) the meaning of our fourth term of unity; (*b*) an outline of the historical argument which justifies that term; (*c*) its practical bearing on the problem of Church Unity.

I.

The fourth term of unity, set forth in 1886, reads: *The Historic Episcopate, locally adapted in the methods of its administration to the varying needs of the nations and peoples called of God into the unity of His Church.**

(*a*) This language is not fairly charged with ambiguity, especially if the nature of the Declaration in which it occurs is considered.† Its leading phrase, "the Historic Episcopate," was surely intended, and has been taken by many, to be simply "the polite equivalent of a controversial term [Apostolic Succession] which had long been in use," as one of our Bishops ‡ expresses it.

---

* Journal Gen. Conv. 1886, p. 80.

† The whole difficulty of interpretation has arisen from isolating the terms of unity from their context.

‡ Bishop McLaren, in the New York *Independent*, Mch. 8, 1894.

But this, the natural interpretation, has been explained away by certain eminent Churchmen, and their explanations have misled certain Protestants and have disturbed many among ourselves who look to the chief Pastors of the Church to give forth no uncertain sound.

Our Bishops are said to have "fastened on certain words, the characteristic of which is, that they express a fact without at all insisting upon any theory of the fact. . . . That government by oversight, which is what 'episcopacy,' when translated, means, has been historically the prevailing method of polity in Christendom, certainly from the second century onwards, is beyond dispute. . . . That if we are to have organic unity at all, it is more reasonable to expect that it should be brought about under this method of pilotage than any other." In short we are told that "it is a simple falling back on fact. Think as you please, the Bishops seem to say, about the nature and sanction of the Christian Ministry." *

We have no quarrel with the amiable spirit which lies behind such an interpretation; but we cannot accept its reasonableness, nor can we discover how the Episcopate will be made more ac-

---

* Dr. Huntington's *Peace of the Church*, pp. 204, 205. Cf. also Dr. Shields's *United Church of the United States*, pp. 5², 1⁻³.

ceptable to Protestant denominations by our refusing to give any more adequate reason for insisting upon it than the fact that it has existed for a long time. Does mere antiquity make a thing necessary? Can the phrase "incapable of compromise or surrender," employed by our Bishops, be rightly applied to anything which is not necessary in itself? Does an opinion on our part that "it is more reasonable to expect that" unity "should be brought about under this method of pilotage than any other" make the Episcopate incapable of compromise or surrender? It is thought, I know, that, if we claim Divine sanction for the Episcopate, we shall be considered presumptuous. But shall we be thought less so in requiring the religious world to yield to us with reference to what we refuse to say is of more than human sanction? Is not humility with those who magnify their office on the ground that it is of Divine institution and held in trust, rather than with those who do the same thing on grounds purely human? Are our Protestant brethren incapable of answering such questions with common sense?

It is indeed true, as even so staunch a Churchman as the late Canon Liddon could say, that, in asserting Apostolic Succession, "we are not formulating a theory, but stating a fact of history."*

---

* *Clerical Life and Work*, pp. 291, 292.

But, as that saintly Priest would readily have agreed, there are facts, of which Apostolic Succession is one, which cannot be stated without immediate implications of doctrinal nature, which we cannot escape without evasion of the facts themselves. Thus, the doubting Thomas found himself obliged, the instant in which he realized the fact that his Master had risen in very flesh and bones from the dead, to acknowledge His Godhead and adore Him; and those who lose their hold upon the reality of the physical resurrection of our Lord come ultimately, if they live long enough, to a denial of His Person. The phrase "Historic Episcopate" stands for a fact of such nature; and the fact signified is that the Episcopate was instituted by Christ to be the earthly source of spiritual jurisdiction and the bond of visible unity in the Church to the end of days.

We cannot accept such a fact without treating the Episcopate as of Divine requirement, and believing that its maintenance is inseparably bound up with the maintenance of true religion. It is as absurd to speak of believing in the Historic Episcopate as a fact merely, as it is to speak of believing in God as a fact merely. God is a Being Whose very Nature requires our loyalty, so that the fact of His existence cannot be duly stated without doctrines and consequences appearing which should modify our lives. In like manner, the

Historic Episcopate is by nature or, if you prefer to put it so, historically, a fact with implications as to authority which we cannot evade without ignoring the contents of the fact itself. The fact includes Christ's mission, and a Divinely sanctioned government in the Church, from which there can be no earthly appeal, as well as a permanent stewardship of grace and truth.

In view of such considerations, we hold that our Bishops were not likely to have submitted the Historic Episcopate " simply as a question of polity," as a brilliant and amiable Presbyterian professor expresses it.* Nor can we assent to his assertion that "it is of prime importance that such dogmas [as Apostolic Succession] . . . should sink out of view while we are considering its claims and merits as a Christian institution." † To require " the Historic Episcopate, as neither enjoining nor forbidding any doctrine of Apostolic Succession"‡ would be mere trifling, whatever our convictions might be. If we look upon the Episcopate as essential to the maintenance of true religion, what right have we to enter into an arrangement which will sooner or later place it in the power of those who regard it as of human origin and subject to human modification? If, on

---

* Prof. Shields's *United Church of the United States*, p. 157.
† Ibid.
‡ Ibid. p. 182.

the other hand, we believe, as we do not, that the Episcopate is merely desirable and not essential, how can we answer satisfactorily the question of the Secretary of the Evangelical Alliance, who asks, "Why make that essential to the organization of all Churches into one, which is conceded to be unessential to the legitimate organization of any?"* Truly "such a position cannot be successfully defended as a *sine qua non* to Church union."† And the light in which thoughtful sectarians usually regard it is truly expressed by a well-known editor, when he says, it "is arrogance, and arrogance is not the road to Christian union."‡

It is, in fact, just such interpretations as I have been reviewing which occasion and justify the charge so frequently made that our insistence upon the Episcopate is the chief barrier to unity.§ We cannot refute such a charge on any other than the highest doctrinal ground, viz., that the Episcopate is of Divine institution and requirement, and for that reason "incapable of compromise or surrender" by its stewards and trustees.

(*b*) To proceed: if our fourth term cannot be cleared from the charge of absurdity except on

---

* Dr Josiah Strong, in *The Question of Unity*, edited by Dr. Bradford, p. 25.
† Ibid. p. 26.
‡ Ibid. p. 38.
§ Ibid. p. 26.

high doctrinal grounds, neither should it be regarded as committing this Church in the slightest degree, unless it is consistent with her formularies. Our Bishops, as they themselves have said recently, speak " not as truth-seekers, but as truth receivers, 'ambassadors in bonds,'" and their "sole inquiry is : What does this Church teach? What is the declaration of God's Holy Word?"[*] Their elevation to the Episcopate did not nullify their priestly obligation and vow " always so to minister the Doctrine and Sacraments, and the Discipline of Christ, as the Lord hath commanded, and as this Church hath received the same." They may indeed say and do much in their episcopal capacity simply, making use of methods not provided for in the Constitution and Canons of our General Convention. They have often done so— "in Council" and in the Lambeth Conferences. But they cannot alter the Constitution and Canons, nor can they lawfully commit the General Convention to the necessity of such alterations, except by methods constitutionally provided.

In view of these elementary principles, we are unwilling to read into the Declaration touching the Historic Episcopate any meaning which would require an alteration in the doctrines of this Church or a change in its polity. No doubt our Bishops will always be ready to do what in them lies to-

---

[*] Pastoral Letter of 1894, p. 9.

ward locally adapting our episcopal polity to the peoples with whom they have to do; but we have too much confidence in them to believe that they will attempt this by unconstitutional methods, inconsistent with the terms on which they have received their Office.* It is hardly necessary to add, that to interpret any part of their Declaration on Unity, issued as it was without legislative action, as intended to commit this Church, under conditions of their own naming, to doctrinal and ecclesiastical changes of radical nature, is to deal somewhat severely with their reputations for loyalty. Surely we are warranted in denying that their language pointed to any "structural surrender";† and in treating their fourth term as intended to be in harmony with the existing formularies and principles of this Church.

Her principles are clear enough in this matter. She has not, indeed, treated her doctrine of the Ministry, or any other portion of her Faith, as requiring legislative enactment, or as affected in the slightest degree as to its binding force by its being inscribed in the Constitution of her General

---

* When they were consecrated they vowed to "exercise such discipline as by the authority of God's Word, and by *the order of this Church*, is committed unto" them. See Ordinal.

† Bishop McLaren, in New York *Independent*, March 8, 1894.

Convention.* It is also true that she has nowhere set forth her doctrine of the Ministry in connected order and detail in her formularies. But we can discover sufficient indications of her mind none the less.

She has said in the Preface of her Ordinal that "from the Apostles' time there have been these Orders of Ministers in Christ's Church, Bishops, Priests and Deacons. Which Offices were evermore had in such reverend estimation, that no man might presume to execute any of them, except he were first called, . . . and also by public Prayer, with Imposition of Hands, were approved and admitted thereunto by lawful Authority. And therefore to the intent that these Orders may be continued, and reverently used and esteemed in this Church, no man shall be accounted or taken to be a lawful Bishop, Priest or Deacon, in this Church, or suffered to execute any of the said functions, except he be called, tried, examined and admitted thereunto, according to the Form hereafter following, or hath had Episcopal Consecra-

---

* The General Convention is not "this Church," but a legal corporation employed by and subject to this Church. Its Constitution is mutable and deals with changeable things. The Church's own Constitution, including her Faith and polity, is divine and immutable. The General Convention legislates for its *maintenance*, not for its enactment, definition, or revision.

tion or Ordination." In her prayers the Church assumes that God has appointed "divers Orders" in His Church, by His "Divine Providence,"* and by His "Holy Spirit";† and that the Apostolic Commission is a proper reason for consecrating Bishops to be the "Pastors" of Christ's Church and to "administer the godly discipline thereof." ‡ She interprets the Scriptural injunction "to lay hands suddenly on no man" as properly applicable to the Consecration of Bishops; § and connects those gifts of the Holy Ghost whereby He makes "some Apostles, some Prophets," etc., with the same action. ‖ She professes "by the imposition of the hands" of her Bishops to confer the Holy Ghost "for the Office and work of a Bishop in the Church of God."

In her Office of Institution she testifies that Christ hath "promised to be with the Ministers of Apostolic Succession to the end of the world." ¶ She receives into her Ministry those who have received Episcopal ordination in other Commun-

---

* Collect in the Ordinal of Deacons.
† Collect in the Ordinal of Priests. Also the prayer before the examination of Bishops-elect.
‡ Collect in the Ordinal of Bishops.
§ Address to the Bishop-elect before his examination.
‖ Prayer before the laying-on of hands. *Cf.* Ephes. iv. 11; I. Cor. xii 28.
¶ Second prayer before the benediction.

ions,* and treats all other so-called ordinations as null and void, in the Constitution and Canons of her General Convention.† In brief, if she has not defined the doctrine of Apostolic Succession in set terms, she has at least tied herself to modes of address to God and man, and to rules of action, which are inscrutable on the supposition that that doctrine does not express her mind.

There has been no reason for formal definitions. This Church is a daughter of the Church of England, being under the Episcopal oversight of the Bishop of London before the Revolution, and asserting her origin and structure by the name Episcopal when the division of national jurisdiction took place. She declares in the Preface of her Prayer Book that she "is far from intending to depart from the Church of England in any essential point of doctrine, discipline or worship." In acting and praying on the basis of the doctrine of Apostolic Succession, therefore, she but retains her ancient constitution and Faith; for, in spite of the vagaries of individual writers and schools and in spite of laxity of individual ecclesiastics in the exercise of discipline, the *corporate position* of the English Church, as embodied in her formularies and displayed in her elaborate care for the preservation of the Historic Episcopate and succession, has

---

* Title I, Canon 15, Digest of 1892.
† Title I., Canon 3 § vi.; *cf.* Canon 17.

been unmistakable, and in agreement with Catholic doctrine.*

(*c*) Having shown to the best of my ability that our fourth term is absurd, presumptuous and disloyal, unless submitted from a high doctrinal point of view, I only need to give explicit proof, by quotations from their own language, that our Bishops were neither unreasonable nor disloyal, but assumed in their fourth term a defensible and Catholic position.

The Declaration consists, as you are aware, of preamble and body. The body of the Declaration includes not only the so-called " terms " of unity (an inaccurate phrase), but also some explanatory matter and an express statement of the *doctrinal reason* for insisting upon the Episcopate and other " terms " of unity. Permit me to quote from it.

We do hereby affirm, our Bishops say, *that the Christian unity now so earnestly desired . . . can be restored only by the return of all Christian Communions to the principles of unity exemplified by the undivided Catholic Church during the first ages of its existence; which principles we believe to be the substantial deposit of Faith and Order committed by Christ and His Apostles to the Church unto the end of the world, and therefore incapable of compromise or surrender by those who have been*

---

* Haddan's *Apostolical Succession*, ch. vi., especially pp. 158-177.

ordained to be its stewards and trustees for the common and equal benefit of all men.

As inherent parts of this sacred deposit, and therefore as essential to the restoration of unity among the divided branches of Christendom, we account the following, to wit:

4. *The Historic Episcopate,** etc.

I have spoken at considerable length on the interpretation of our fourth term of unity, because I am convinced that the novelties which have been imputed to our Bishops will do more harm to the cause of genuine Church Unity, if allowed to pass, than can be repaired for a long time to come. I think, however, that I need not say more in connection with this, except to give a brief outline of the sense in which our fourth term appears to be submitted.

1. That term, so far as it may be called a term, is an *ultimatum*, for our Bishops declare that the Episcopate is "incapable of compromise or surrender."

2. The reason advanced for thus insisting upon the Episcopate is that it is an "inherent part" of a "sacred deposit," "the substantial deposit of Faith and Order committed by Christ and His Apostles to the Church unto the end of the world."

3. The Catholic doctrine of the Episcopate is not

---

* Gen. Conv. Journal, 1886, p. 80.

expressly mentioned among our terms of unity;* but the reason given for offering the terms which are mentioned, and, therefore, the *sense* in which the Historic Episcopate is insisted upon, make it impossible to accept the fourth term in good faith without accepting that doctrine.

4. No action has been contemplated by this Church which would be likely, at any future time, to render the maintenance of the traditional position and doctrine of the Episcopate an open question.

Let us pass on.

II.

The second part of my task is to give an outline of the historical argument by which our fourth term of unity may be defended.

We need not concern ourselves with the abstract question as to whether it is the *being* or the *well-being* of the Church that makes the Episcopate essential; for, if it is essential to either, it must be "incapable of compromise or surrender." Our position is not based upon abstract distinctions, but is historical, and consists in the belief that the Historic Episcopate was ordained by Christ and His Apostles, and given the exclusive jurisdiction and power of self-perpetuation by im-

---

* So Prof. Shields urges in his *United Church*, p. 184.

position of hands, which is still conceded to it by three-fourths of the Christian world.

(*a*) The time at my disposal will not admit of my attempting more than to give an outline of our historical argument, and to point out the significance of its various parts.

At the outset, permit me to call your attention to the limits of what should be expected of us in defending our position. *The burden of proof does not rest upon our shoulders.* Our position is historically far more ancient than any which opposes it, and has been maintained by the Catholic Church without interruption from the earliest age to which it is possible to retrace the continuity of Christian thought and practice. From that age until the Protestant revolution of modern days no departure from this position occurred worth mentioning. Moreover, the original Protestant bodies did not break away from the Episcopate intentionally or on principle in the first instance, but invented the presbyterial and congregational theories of ecclesiastical polity, *ex post facto*, in order to justify their continuance in the state of schism into which their unregulated zeal for reform had brought them.* In common with a vast majority of living Christians, we have inherited the mind of the saints through many unbroken ages; and until positive evidence is forthcoming, sufficient to show

---

* Haddan's *Apostolical Succession*, pp. 101, 131–137.

that this mind was not the pentecostal mind of the Church, nor that of sub-apostolic Christianity, the paths of safety for us will be what we have known to be the ancient paths.

Various attempts have been made to prove that Episcopacy was not established by Christ and His Apostles, but was of subsequent and purely human development. They all fall into two classes.

1. The first class of arguments makes much of names, and treats the terms Bishop, Presbyter and Deacon as if they possessed from the outset a fixed and technical meaning such as they acquired at a later period. On this assumption it is argued that when St. Paul speaks of Timothy's ordination "with the laying on of the hands of the presbytery,"* he means that Timothy was ordained by those whom we in our day would call Presbyters. Again, it is alleged, on slender grounds, that in sub-apostolic days the Bishop of Alexandria was appointed and ordained by Presbyters.†

Without entering into details, it is a sufficient

---

* I. Tim. iv. 14.

† Lightfoot, *Dissertations on Apostolic Age*, p. 194, in his anxiety to avoid claiming too much, appears to concede this. But Gore, *On the Ministry*, pp. 134-144, and Note B, discusses Lightfoot's reasons and shows that his concession was uncalled for.

answer to both instances alleged to say that the use of ministerial titles was too fluctuating in primitive days to be made the basis of argument, unless circumstances can be shown to indicate the particular application of the title which is employed in the instances cited. As Bishop Andrewes has shown, " in the beginning regard was not had to distinction of names; the authority and power was ever distinct, the name not restrained, either in this, or other."* The Apostles themselves were called Bishops, † Presbyters ‡ and Deacons. § The successors of the Apostles, whom we call Bishops, were also called in the New Testament Apostles,‖ Presbyters ¶ and Deacons.** Those who belonged apparently to the Order below the Bishops were called Bishops also.†† Our Lord Himself was called Apostle,‡‡ Bishop,§§ Priest ‖‖ and Deacon.¶¶ Surely an argument which depends for its force upon the use of a ministerial title in the New Testament must be valueless, unless supported by conclusive evidence

---

* *A Summary View of the Government, Both of the Old and New Testament.* Ang. Cath. Ly., pp. 359, 360.
  † Acts i. 20.
  ‡ I. Pet. v. 1.
  § I. Cor. iii. 5.
  ‖ Phil. ii. 25.
  ¶ I Tim. v. 17.
  ** I. Tim. iv. 6.
  †† Phil. i. 1; Tit. i. 7.
  ‡‡ Heb. iii. 1.
  §§ I. Pet. ii. 25.
  ‖‖ Heb. v. 6.
  ¶¶ Rom. xv. 8.

as to the application of the title in the case referred to. This lack of fixed and technical use of names continued for some time after the death of the Apostles in certain portions of the Church, and may be held to account sufficiently for the apparent anomalies in Alexandria and elsewhere.

The Church did not hold the doctrine of the Trinity with less faithfulness in ante-Nicene days, because she had not yet learned to express its contents with the theological accuracy which she acquired by conflict with heretical subtleties.* In like manner, we may not argue that the Church failed to distinguish the Episcopate from the Presbyterate, or that she did not recognize its exclusive authority and Divine sanction, merely because she had not yet acquired that caution and crystallized accuracy in the use of titles which is the result of experience alone.

2. The other line of argument is one which was used with great skill by the late Dr. Hatch.† It was not original with him, although by no one more plausibly presented, but has been frequently urged by Protestant writers. Dr. Hatch argued as follows: The phenomena of Christian history

---

* Bishop Bull and Newman have shown this.

† *The Organization of the Early Christian Churches:* being the Bampton Lectures of 1880.

are undoubtedly unique in their transcendent interest and importance: "but if they or any part of them [*e.g.*, those connected with Episcopacy] can be accounted for by causes which are known to have operated in the production of similar phenomena, under similar conditions of society, the presumption, in the absence of positive evidence to the contrary, will be in favour of those who infer an identity of cause,"* and claim that the episcopal polity of the Church is of natural origin and accounted for by that "economy of causes" by which the whole universe is governed. He urges that it is not legitimate to allow an *a priori* theory of what God was likely to do to override the conclusions which follow from an examination of what He has actually done.† Yet his own argument is made illegitimate by the very mistake which he criticises. He honestly acknowledges "the disadvantage under which any one labours who declines the short and easy road" which an acceptance of the traditional hypothesis "seems to offer"; and admits that "a hypothesis has long been current which does not admit of direct refutation, and which assigns the origin of this quasi-monarchical government to an institution of our Lord or the Apostles acting under His express

---

* Bampton Lectures, pp. xix , 17-19.
† Ibid. pp. 213-216.

directions." He prefers, however, to "wind his way through a dense undergrowth of facts," as he calls them, saying that "it is impossible"—I quote his words—"to accept the belief that the Episcopate forms an exception to the general course of the divine government of the world, and to refrain from proceeding to the inquiry whether any causes were in operation which are adequate to account for its supremacy, without resorting to the hypothesis of a special and extraordinary institution."*

The argument is, as I have said, skilfully worked out. Each phenomenon is treated as if belonging entirely to the natural order, and made to bear a different meaning from that which it admits of when regarded from the traditional point of view. Conjecture is made to do the work of ascertained fact, and an hypothesis is built up which may appear plausible to those who accept the author's *a priori* assumption, in favor of which he cannot himself claim anything stronger than presumption. The validity of the argument depends entirely upon the validity of its assumption that Episcopacy cannot have been of supernatural origin and Divine institution. This assumption begs the question, and is the same in kind with that of Hume in his argument against miracles—the im-

---

* Bampton Lectures, p. 84.

possibility of supernatural interventions in history. The method is that of Gibbon,* who thought he had accounted for the origin of Christianity on natural grounds when he had marshalled an array of facts, partly real and partly conjectural, which might under conceivable conditions have led to the rise of something like Christianity without miraculous aid. No one but a rationalist could adopt such a method of argument after discerning its real nature.†

It remains true, therefore, that, until rationalism

---

* *Decline and Fall*, ch. xv.

† Two remarks may well be added:

(*a*) Dr. Hatch bases his argument somewhat on analogy. He argues that the term *episcopos*, for example, was applied to certain executive officials among the heathen, who had to do with the finances of the bodies which appointed them (pp. 37, 38). Corresponding officials in the Christian Churches, he urges would naturally receive the same title. This *might* be so. But, waiving the question as to whether it was so, the Christian *episcopos* would not *for that reason* be merely a financial executive. It is to be remembered that we are not concerned with the origin of the *name* "Episcopos," but with the origin, nature and sanction of the Christian *Office* which came to be called by that name.

(*b*) Dr. Hatch altogether ignores the historical indications contained in the New Testament, urging the uncertainty of its interpretation and insinuating the doubtfulness of the date of the Pastoral Epistles (pp. 20-23). Such a defect must of course distort his premises and make his conclusions worthless.

becomes preferable to a belief in the possibility of miracles, the traditional hypothesis that Episcopacy was instituted by "our Lord or the Apostles acting under His express directions" is not capable of refutation. *The burden of proof remains with our opponents.*

(*b*) If we were concerned with self-defence merely we might rest content. But it is our duty to persuade men of the truth, and, if possible, to bring back those who have wandered away, so that they may share with us in the inestimable blessings which are dispensed by the true Ministry of Christ. I shall endeavor, therefore, to give an outline of our argument on its positive side. The materials for this argument are becoming richer as the darkness which has hitherto veiled the period following the death of St. Paul is being partially dissipated. They consist of ascertained facts; and each new fact, so far as it bears on the question, fits in with and therefore strengthens the traditional and accepted belief of the Church.

Our argument consists, in the main, of four particulars:

1. In the first place, we learn from the New Testament that our Lord did, as a matter of fact, institute a Ministry, to which He ordained His Apostles, and endowed it with the powers which belonged by the Father's appointment to His own

Ministry.* We also find permanent duties and promises attached to the Ministry thus instituted, such as could not be fulfilled except on the supposition that there was to be an Apostolic Succession of the Ministry until the end of days.†

2. In the next place, it is clear that, before passing away, the Apostles imparted to others their ordinary ministerial powers, as distinguished from extraordinary and miraculous ones, by laying on of hands—not with the same completeness in every instance, but in such wise that, before the death of St. Paul, three Orders of the Ministry had been instituted, similar to those which we now call the Episcopate, the Presbyterate and the Diaconate.‡ The names of these Orders were, of course, unfixed at first; but the realities corresponding to the names Bishop, Priest, and Deacon appear so unmistakably in the Pastoral Epistles that some critics have made use of the fact to throw doubt upon the Pauline authorship of these Epistles.§

In this Ministry we find the power of ordaining,

---

* St. Mark iii. 14; St. John xv. 16; St. Matt. xxviii. 18; St. John xx. 21.

† St. Mark xvi. 15; St. Matt. x. 23; xxviii. 20.

‡ This is well shown in Eagar's little book, *The Christian Ministry in the New Testament*, S. P. C. K.

§ *Cf.* Liddon's *Clerical Life and Work*, pp. 296, 297. For an unanswerable defence of these Epistles see Hort's *Judaistic Christianity*, ch. vii.

which distinguishes our Bishops from inferior Ministers, lodged in the hands of successors of the Apostles,* which successors have rule over the Presbyters and are the guardians of the Faith and Order of the Church.† There is not the slightest evidence of any upward development of the Ministry in New Testament days. The highest Order —the Apostolate—appears first, and the Apostles ruled the Church by reason of a commission and ordination from above simply. The Church continued to be governed either by the Apostles or by those whom the Apostles ordained for the oversight. It is true, as Lightfoot says, that Timothy's relation to the Church of Ephesus appears to have been temporary; ‡ yet, as he also shows, the nature and functions of his ministry were episcopal, and such that the clergy of Ephesus were placed under him, although some of them appear to have been his seniors in age.§ The position of St. James in Jerusalem was also that of a Bishop, ruling over the Presbyters and inferior clergy. ‖ The localization of the Episcopate and the development of sees and provinces

---

* Liddon, pp. 298, 299.
† Eagar, pp. 28 *et seq.*
‡ *Dissertations on the Apostolic Age*, p. 157.
§ Ibid., p. 158.
‖ Ibid., pp. 155, 156. *Cf.* Acts xii. 17; xv. 13 *et seq.*; xxi. 18; Gal. i. 19; ii. 9, 12.

was gradual; and, however important for the preservation of ecclesiastical order, was clearly left to be determined and, when necessary, modified to suit the conditions and circumstances of "the nations and peoples called of God into the unity of His Church."

3. The third particular of our argument is that, so soon as the Church of sub-Apostolic days emerges into historical view, so that its universal Order can be discerned with certainty—a period not later than the third decade of the second century *—it appears as possessing a threefold Ministry like that which is seen in the Pastoral Epistles, and which is held to be of Divine institution and requirement. This Ministry and this doctrine of it has continued without interruption to the present day †; and is what our Bishops have named as essential to the restoration of unity.

4. Finally, we argue that such facts and indications as are available in studying the period concerning which our present information is less adequate—say from 68 to 130 A.D.—all fit in with and

---

* Lightfoot, pp. 143, 160; Schaff's *Reunion of Christendom* (Evang. Alliance Doc. xxxiii.), p. 23.

† Dr. Davenport has shown, in a lecture before this Club (Series of 1890, Lec. v., pp. 193 *et seq.*), how absolutely free from question and from need of support by canon law the position of the Episcopate was during the period of the Ecumenical Councils.

some directly confirm the hypothesis that the Ministry which emerges to our view early in the second century not only agrees with that which St. Paul recognized and which the Apostles established in Jerusalem, but is a continuance of it in accordance with Apostolic provision. This ground has often been travelled over. St. Clement of Rome, writing to the Corinthians not later than 95 A.D., distinctly alleges that the Apostles had made provision for a continuance of the Episcopal Office.* The evidence that St. John became Bishop of Ephesus and Metropolitan of the first ecclesiastical province before his death, which occurred about 100 A.D., is fairly conclusive; and it is in keeping with this that, in the Apocalypse, he is charged by Christ with messages to the Angels of the Seven Churches in the province of Asia.† These Angels are most easily interpreted to be Bishops of the Churches named.‡ About ten years after the death of St. John § occurs the emphatic testimony of St. Ignatius of Antioch as to the necessity of Bishops, Presbyters and Deacons to the organization of any true Church,‖ and

---

* *St. Clem. ad Cor.*, ch. xliv.

† Chapters i.-iii.

‡ Trench, *On the Epistles to the Seven Churches*, pp. 55–61, 4th edit.

§ Lightfoot's *Apostolic Fathers*, edit. 1889; P. II., Vol. II., pp. 435–472.

‖ *Ad Mag. 13; ad Tral. 3, 7; ad Phil. 4, ad Smyr. 8.*

his assertion that this Ministry fills the place occupied by Christ and His Apostles during our Lord's earthly Ministry.* The genuineness of the letters in which this testimony occurs has been completely established by the late Bishop Lightfoot.† Perfect lists of the successors of the Apostles in various cities are preserved in the writings of Eusebius and others.‡ Not one undoubted fact can be alleged against this evidence; and we might as well believe that the river which emerges from the mists beneath the Niagara Falls is a different stream from that which flows over them, as to suppose that the Ministry which has come down to us from the second century is other than that which the Apostles received from Christ and transmitted to their immediate successors. Not one trace remains of that mighty revolution which is said to have imposed a new Ministry of non-apostolic and purely human origin upon the entire Church, and to have convinced those who had been taught at the feet of the Apostles themselves that this novelty was of Divine and Apostolic institution.§

The evidence for the genuineness of the New

---

* *Ad Ephes.* 6; *ad Mag.* 6; *ad Tral.* 2.
† *Apostolic Fathers*, edit. 1889; P. II., Vol. I., pp. 328-430.
‡ Gore, *On the Ministry*, pp. 128-134, 161-163; edit. 1889; Lightfoot, *On the Ministry* (*Diss. Ap. Age*), pp. 168 *et seq.*
§ *Cf.* Haddan's *Apostolical Succession*, pp. 104-124.

Testament Scriptures is not so complete* as is the proof that "from the Apostles' time there have been these Orders in Christ's Church—Bishops, Priests and Deacons," of Divine sanction and requirement, and perpetuated by means of the laying on of hands of the Historic Episcopate. †

(*c*) Before passing on, it will be well to review very briefly some of the objections which have been made in order to break the force of such historical evidence.

1. It is said, for example, that Apostolic Succession necessarily requires elaborate proof, so elaborate, in fact, that comparatively few Christians are in a position to master its details. It is unlikely, our separated brethren urge, that God has imposed upon men the duty of obedience to a Ministry the authority of which is so difficult to establish. This objection ignores the circumstance that the burden of proof rests upon those who reject the Episcopate, and not upon those who obey it. The authority of the Episcopate did not require elaborate proof in primitive days,

---

* *Cf.* Haddan's *Apostolical Succession*, pp. 125-128.

† At the conclusion of his argument on the Christian Ministry, *Dissertation on Apostolic Age*, pp. 235, 236, Bishop Lightfoot says: "If the preceding investigation be substantially correct, the three-fold Ministry can be traced to Apostolic direction; and short of an express statement we can possess no better assurance of a divine appointment, or at least a divine sanction."

and it has ever since enjoyed that kind of possession which constitutes "nine points of the law," and which still secures the obedience of three-fourths of Christendom. The difficulties which are said to surround a proof of its claims are felt only by sectarians, and are due, not to any intrinsic doubtfulness attendant upon them, but to the disorders caused by the rise and continuance of sectarianism. It is this sectarianism which requires elaborate proof for its justification, not the claims of the Church's historic Ministry.*

2. Again, the phrase "tactual succession" is seized upon, and we are charged with setting store by mere externals instead of rejoicing in that spiritual succession which is independent of externals.† But the force of such an objection depends upon two misapprehensions—viz., that tactual succession, as it is called, is a device of ours; and that we prize it as a substitute for the invisible work of the Spirit. We hold that it is Christ Who has willed to authenticate His Ministry in this manner from age to age, in order to prevent spiritual anarchy and to provide visible tokens of the validity of the Ministry appointed to represent Him until the end of days. Furthermore, we value this succession, not in isolation

---

* *Cf.* Haddan's *Apostolical Succession*, pp. 61-69.

† The late Bishop Brooks raised this objection at one of our Church Congresses.

from, nor as a substitute for, the work of God's Holy Spirit, but as an appointed *means* whereby the Spirit achieves His work in the Church. If many who yield external conformity to the Ministry are unspiritual, it is because they misuse the Ministry. Those, on the other hand, who strain after spiritual results apart from it, end in devising substitutes for it which are equally external, but lack Divine sanction and promise. The objection to tactual succession is in reality a branch of the objection against the sacramental idea; and, if valid, would militate against all of the dispensation of grace wrapped up in the taking of flesh by Him Who came to save our flesh.*

3. We are told, however, that what is objected to is not so much the Episcopate itself as the superadded notion of exclusive privilege,† the putting of an Order of men between the soul and God, and the unchurching of those denominations which do not possess the Historic Episcopate. It is sufficient to reply that what is termed exclusive privilege is simply *stewardship*, instituted by God. No doubt the stewards are quite unworthy, but certainly, as the Bishop of Ohio says, it is not the fault of the Episcopal Church "that

---

* *Cf.* Bishop Seymour's *Historic Episcopate*, Vol. I., No. 1 of *Church Unity Quarterly*, pp. 19-22; also Haddan's *Apostolical Succession*, pp. 32, 33, 49-51.

† Geo. A. Gates, D.D., in Bradford's *Question of Unity*, p. 47.

this Ministry is her inheritance. The burden was imposed too long ago, and has been borne for too many generations to be objected to now at this end of the nineteenth century."* We are indeed convinced that no denominations can lawfully claim the name Church without the Apostolic Ministry, but to say that we have done the un-churching is not in harmony with the facts of history.† The Church's Ministry does not put itself between the soul and God, but is Christ's instrument for bringing souls to Himself.‡ It is hardly necessary to add that we do not judge Protestants. Unavoidable ignorance and unfortunate conditions account for many things; and God is manifestly blessing many in spite of sad mistakes. He is not limited by His instruments in every case, but *men are*, when they are able to discover them.

4. Another objection is drawn from the fact that the Church is an organism and grows. Why, it is urged, should not such a thing conform to the law of growing things and change, as it matures?§ The answer is simple. The changes

---

* Bishop Leonard in the New York *Independent*, March 8, 1894.

† Bishop Seymour's *Historic Episcopate*, p. 13; Haddan's *Apostolical Succession*, pp. 58–61; Gore, *The Ministry*, pp. 109–111, 344–348.

‡ Haddan's *Apostolical Succession*, pp. 41–49.

§ Wm. Cooley, in *The Question of Unity*, pp. 41, 42.

which the higher organisms undergo in their growth do not affect the structural type when that is once developed. The Church's Ministry pertains to her structural type. Once developed, it never can change in constitution, whatever may be the growth and superficial developments in the Church. Structural change would originate a new organism. It could not perpetuate the old.

Neither these nor any other difficulties will trouble men after they realize that Christianity is something more than a philosophy or set of opinions. There are principles, indeed, and a " Faith once for all delivered " which we must preserve; but the Church is a dispenser of sacramental grace as well as of doctrine, and the maintenance of the Faith itself depends upon the continuance of that Ministry which was ordained by Christ to bear witness in His Name.*

III.

We have now to consider the bearing of our Bishops' position on the Church Unity problem.

(*a*) You will, of course, agree with me when I say that it is our duty to promote a restoration of the visible unity of the Church. Such unity would make it possible to do much which has hitherto been impracticable, in overcoming religious indif-

---

* Haddan's *Apostolical Succession*, pp. 55-58.

ference at home and in converting the heathen abroad. And such unity is to be sought, not merely as a means, but as *an end in itself*, since visible unity signifies visible charity, the very chief of Christian graces, and our Lord Himself prayed for its maintenance in the solemn night of His betrayal.*

The Protestants of our day did not originate sectarianism, although they have, none the less, inherited a schismatic position. We need not be blaming them, therefore, when we say that the nature and genesis of their position hinders them from appreciating as Churchmen do the sinful nature of schism † and the necessity of adopting the right course, however difficult, for its removal. There is considerable talk of unity in the air, and many noble utterances have been made; but we err greatly if we think that our separated brethren understand what true Church Unity is and involves, or that any widespread yearning exists among them for the restoration of unity.

We ought not to blame them for this limitation of vision, caused as it is by remote circumstances. Yet, while bound to be courteous and kind, we are bound to be true and candid. We may not help to perpetuate or acquiesce in the existing ig-

---

* St. John xvii. 21. Cf. Dr. Shields's *United Church*, p. 117.
† Dr. Schaff, *Reunion of Christendom*, pp. 8–14, is a good example of this failure. Cf. Bradford's *Question of Unity*, p 7.

norance of separatists as to the real meaning of their position, the sinfulness of schism, and the course necessary to be pursued in order to restore visible unity and charity.*

(*b*) It is from such a point of view that our Bishops have declared the Historic Episcopate to be "essential to the restoration of unity among the divided branches of Christendom." Their purpose, if I mistake not, was *didactic*. They were not making demands. Strictly speaking, they were not offering terms, so much as exercising the prophetic Office which Christ gave to His Apostolic Ministry and which they may not neglect to exercise when proper occasions arrive. Certain memorials addressed to them concerning the necessity of facing the problem of Church Unity moved them to declare by way of instruction to all who would listen, not what they chose to demand, but some of the things which, under any circumstances, are *essential* to the restoration of unity. Among these things they named the Historic Episcopate. They expressed or implied three ***reasons for*** its necessity, but neither stated nor implied their own choice as having anything to do with the matter.

1. The first of these reasons† is that the Epis-

---

* Bradford's *Question of Unity*, pp. 20, 21.

† I have discussed these reasons elsewhere in my pamphlet, *The Historic Position of the Episcopal Church*, Young Churchman Co., Milwaukee, pp. 56-61.

copate is an inherent part of "the substantial deposit of Faith and Order committed by Christ and His Apostles to the Church unto the end of the world." The question at issue here is not one of mere human polity, subject to possible modification, but one which relates to the permanent structure and organic continuity of the Church of God, and to the preservation of the Faith and of the covenanted means of grace.* To surrender the Episcopate would not church the sects, but would unchurch ourselves and originate one more sect to gladden the arch-enemy of Christ's Kingdom. † And even should such surrender end in the unification of non-episcopal bodies, it would not secure Church Unity, but would bring to birth a new thing —a huge kingdom of men, differing in kind from the Church for whose unity Christ prayed. The Church is a *living and unchangeable organism*, founded and inhabited by the Holy Ghost, and no combination of *human organizations* can ever take its place or perform its functions. ‡

2. Two other reasons for the necessity of the Historic Episcopate are implied when our Bishops say that unity " can be restored only by the return

---

* *Cf.* Bp. Jackson, New York *Independent*, Mch. 3, 1894.

† *Cf.* Bp. Tuttle, New York *Independent*, Mch. 8, 1894.

‡ This mode of statement comes to me from one of our missionaries abroad, whose sense of its truth is intensified by his missionary experience.

of all Christian Communions to the principles of unity exemplified by the undivided Catholic Church during the first ages of its existence."

The first of these is that the Historic Episcopate is the only Ministry which has ever held the Church together in visible unity. This is too plain to need special argument. The ancient Church was visibly one, and was governed by the Episcopate, each Bishop representing the whole Episcopal College in his own jurisdiction.* The encroachments of the papal system, by which the Episcopate was displaced in effect, if not in theory,† cut Christendom in twain ; ‡ and the development of presbyterial and congregational polities originated the countless divisions which confront us in this land. §

---

* St. Cyprian, in his treatise *On the Unity of the Church*, says: "The Episcopate is one; it is a whole, in which each enjoys full possession" (ch. 4). Library of the Fathers, Oxford,

† Dr. Bright, *Waymarks of History*, p. 207, reminds us that even the Vatican decree bears witness to "that ordinary power of episcopal jurisdiction whereby Bishops, who, being placed by the Holy Spirit, have succeeded in the room of the Apostles, act as true pastors," etc.

‡ The Pope excommunicated the East in 1054, and the *Ecclesia Anglicana* in the time of Elizabeth. To the last-named act no retort in kind has ever been made.

§ *Cf.* Bps. Boyd Vincent and Graves, in New York *Independent*, Mch. 8, 1894. Prof. Shields. *United Church*, pp. 89-93, exhibits the unifying power of the Episcopate.

3. Finally, our Bishops imply that to ask us to surrender the Episcopate is to ask what would be altogether ineffectual unless we could draw after us those bodies which, like this body, have inherited the Ministry of the ancient and undivided Church and regard it as "incapable of compromise or surrender." If two-thirds of professing Christians still continue to maintain Episcopacy, a surrender on our part will accomplish nothing for unity;* but will simply put us into the sectarian camp, and deprive us forever of our mission of reclaiming those who have wandered away from the covenanted ministry of grace and truth.† We may not, even for the sake of reclaiming others, reduce ourselves to the necessity of being reclaimed. Those who ask us to surrender the Episcopate do not perceive the world-wide scope of the problem of unity,‡ and the impossibility that measures which violate the religious convictions of the bulk of the Christian world should be otherwise than a hindrance to ultimate unity.

(c) At this point it may be well to notice certain schemes for the unification of denominations in this land; schemes which recognize that a place

---

* Bp. Doane, New York *Independent*, Mch. 8, 1894, shows that we cannot act apart from the English Church.

† *Cf.* Bp. Niles, New York *Independent*, Mch. 8, 1894; Bradford's *Question of Unity*, p. 8

‡ I believe Bp. Coxe has pointed this out.

must be allowed for episcopal polity, considered simply as polity, but which have the common fault, as I shall try to show, of involving compromise of principle on our part.*

1. First in order is the *Confederation* scheme, which would not involve the destruction of existing denominations, but merely their federation under a General Conference on the basis of the four terms of unity, but without any alteration in denominational standards or polities, beyond what would be necessary for conformity to the four terms, apart from any doctrinal interpretation of them. This scheme assumes that nothing more is needed to put a sectarian body in a position to be treated with and united with on equal terms† than a readiness on its part to adopt the "Quadrilateral" in the lowest and most external sense which can be read into it. In short, it means that the Church of the future shall make an open question of every Catholic dogma and principle which is not expressly guarded in the Quadrilateral when isolated from the rest of the Declaration on Unity.

2. Next is the *Consolidation* or Constitutional Amendment scheme, which means that the Quadrilateral, without interpretative matter of any kind, shall be put into the preamble or main body of

---

* I borrow my data in this discussion chiefly from Prof. Shields's *United Church*, pp. 93 *et seq.*

† *Cf.* Bradford's *Question of Unity,* pp. 14, 16.

the Constitution of our General Convention, and that such legislation shall be gradually accomplished as will reduce the obligatory principles of doctrine, discipline, worship and polity in the Church to the level of the Quadrilateral as thus limited.* This assumes that our Bishops set forth their four terms as a complete list of the things which are " incapable of compromise or surrender," so that Confirmation, for example, may be treated as non-essential.† If they meant this, they meant something subversive of Christianity. I, for one, do not believe it ‡

3. Finally, there is the *organic growth* scheme, as it is called, which does not look to any present disturbance of denominational lines, but to a series of concurrent ordinations, in which no doctrinal issues are to be raised, but a ministry is to be created in the denominations, the validity of which all will recognize; this to be followed by a regulated reciprocity of pulpits and increasing mutual approximation until all grounds of separation disappear.§ Apart from its visionary character, the

---

* Huntington's *Peace of the Church*, pp. 231 *et seq.*

† *Cf.* Heb. vi. 2.

‡ It is often objected that we should not allow non-essentials to keep us apart. But the very question at issue is, " What is essential and what non-essential ?"

§ Dr. Shields's plan. *United Church*, pp. 99 *et seq.*, 204 *et seq.*

plan assumes that doctrinal questions can be waived lawfully by the Church, and that our Bishops can consecrate to an Office instituted by Christ for the maintenance of the Faith those who are expressly permitted to substitute modern systems for the original " Faith once for all delivered to the saints."

An important distinction needs to be mentioned in connection with this. I mean that between *toleration* and *permission.* The Church is required to maintain the true Faith against every form of " erroneous and strange doctrine contrary to God's Word." Therefore she cannot permit, or in any manner *connive at*, heretical teaching on the part of those whom she ordains with the laying on of hands.* She may indeed *tolerate* much imperfect faith and error, not as making such error *lawful*, but as refraining for the moment from disciplining what is *unlawful*, when the general maintenance of truth is not imperiled thereby and when immediate discipline would quench a smoking flax and produce greater evils than it would cure. No doubt many Bishops have been too lax in the exercise of discipline, and have shown more regard for the feelings of heretics than for those of the faithful. May God forgive them! But such abuses

---

* There are some excellent observations on this subject in Bp. Creighton's recent book on *Persecution and Tolerance*, the last lecture.

pale into insignificance beside the proposal to advance throngs of preachers to the Priesthood with the distinct understanding that they may continue to preach the anti-sacerdotal and anti-Catholic systems of doctrine which they have hitherto adopted. This would be more than *toleration* of error. It would be giving a recognized place to heresy in that Ministry which was ordained for its overthrow. It would be treason against Him Who is the Author and Finisher of our Faith.*

My task is nearly finished, and I have nothing to add except by way of concluding this series of lectures on Church Unity.

(*a*) The Declaration on Unity has been taken to signify a change of ecclesiastical position, and to contain proposals looking towards a possible course of action hitherto unthought of by this Church. In reality it was put forth, not to advertise or propose a new departure, but in order to exhibit certain ancient principles for which this Church has always stood. Our Bishops said nothing inconsistent with their traditional position when they summed up the things essential in the phrase, "the principles of unity exemplified by the undivided Catholic Church during the first ages

---

* Heb. xii. 2. Bp. Whipple shows that we may not substitute courtesy for principle ; and Bp. Whitehead is unable to discern any good results likely to follow upon a yielding contrary to conviction. New York *Independent*, Mch. 8, 1894.

of its existence." Furthermore, the four terms, so-called, were not named as the *sum total* of these essential principles,* but as *parts* simply; parts, it is true, which, if accepted in the sense which the body of the Declaration requires, involve and lead on to all the rest. This Church does not propose to achieve unity either by levelling down, or by any novel platform or procedure; but by levelling up, and by a return to the ancient paths. And the principles which she insists upon are not peculiar to what is called the Protestant Episcopal denomination, but have been maintained by the Catholic Church of every age and race. They are maintained by this Church because she is a true Communion of the Catholic Church.

(*b*) This attitude represents *principles* and *convictions* which are bound up with the very being of the Church, and derives its outspoken character from the belief that the structural principles of a Church which God thought worthy of purchasing with His own Blood are worth proclaiming, and that truth and candor make for unity and charity.†
Our Bishops meant to express themselves clearly,

---

* Prof. Shields appears to think that they were. *United Church*, pp. 130, 188.

† Open assertion can never be "infelicitous" when silence would be misleading, unless the *manner* is infelicitous. *Cf.* Prof. Shields, *United Church*, pp. 150-153.

and did so exp ess themselves. It is not their fault that their words have been misunderstood.

(*c*) My brethren, the visible unity of the Church will come in due time. God speed the day! And we can hasten the time, provided we are faithful to " the principles of unity exemplified by the undivided Catholic Church during the first ages of its existence"; not otherwise. Novel schemes and forced measures will not secure or hasten the result. A contradiction of principles exists which can be remedied only by a change of convictions on the part of those who have forsaken the ancient paths.* Disguise it though we may, there must be surrender—not by compulsion, nor to men, but by conversion, and to God and His ancient Church.

I do not look for any such surrender on the part of sectarian bodies, although God may bring even this to pass. It is more likely that individual wanderers will discover the true way, provided those who are under obligation to proclaim it have the courage of their convictions and the charity which is true, and return to that centre of unity —the Historic Episcopate—from which their fathers departed. If I am right, Church Unity

---

* Protestants naturally fail to realize this. See Prof. Shields, pp. 81-83. 7-31, 12); Shaff on *Reunion*, pp. 2-4. But *cf*. Bradford's *Question of Unity*, p. 25.

will result from a survival of the fittest—*i.e.*, the Divine—and from purer and richer catholicity in what survives, such as will prove beyond doubt that there is a common Faith and Order in the Catholic Church. Then will the different branches of Christendom recognize that they belong to one family, and should endeavor "to keep the unity of the Spirit in the bond of peace"; for "there is one Body, and one Spirit, even as ye are called in one hope of your calling; one Lord, one Faith, one Baptism, one God and Father of all, Who is above all, and through all, and in you all."

It seems scarcely necessary to say that the Church Club is not responsible for any individual opinions on points not ruled by the Church, which the learned theologians who have been good enough to lecture under its auspices may have expressed.

www.ingramcontent.com/pod-product-compliance
Lightning Source LLC
Chambersburg PA
CBHW020908230426
43666CB00008B/1358